As Time Goes By

My Life Story

Robert "Bob" D. Green

ISBN: 1985202352
ISBN-13: 978-1985202351

DEDICATION

To my wife, Sandy,
in gratitude for her loving support.

Table of Contents

Chapter 1   Family

I was born on August 21, 1926, in Syracuse, New York, and I believe my uncle, Thaddeus Oot, was the doctor attending. My father was Raymond V. Green, a Fultonian, and my mother was Edith Eleanor Oot. Edith was from Minoa and moved to Fulton when she married. Her parents were from Germany, but spoke broken English.

Four generations of Greens. L to R: my great-grandfather Samuel, uncle Fred, cousin Clara and grandfather James.

My dad had two brothers. The oldest was Fred; he did paperhanging, painting, etc. I remember when we were younger he and his wife used to come to our house on a Sunday, driving his Model T Ford Sedan. He had his large collie riding on the running board. As he pulled into the yard, I would run and hide from the dog, as I was scared of it. Later, when they were all in the house visiting, we children would play in the car. He didn't care because everything in the car was safe. Dad had a younger sister, Clara, who died at the age of 16 years old of scarlet fever. My dad's other brother, Harry, was instrumental in continuing my family's tradition, Green's Candy.

My dad had his heart set on going to college, but his father didn't think a college education was necessary. Dad was determined anyway and ended up going to Rensselaer Polytechic Institute, enrolled in engineering and successfully finished earned his degree. My brothers would tell about how Dad owned an electronic store with a partner. Eventually, the partner backed out and dad eventually lost the store and a lot of money. My only recollection of his career was of his working at Victoria Mills as a plant engineer.

Above, Dad in a Curtiss-Wright Airplane. Right, Dad (second from left) as a captain in the Oswego County Civil Air Patrol, a support system for the U.S. Army Air Force.

My dad was a professional engineer at the Victoria Paper Mill in Fulton. He also did a lot of engineering at other paper mills in the area, such as North End in Fulton and Sweet in Phoenix. He did a lot of traveling for the Victoria Paper Mill, looking for parts. When he was about to leave on one of these trips, I remember telling him to speed there and back as I would miss him while he was gone. My dad would take me with him on some of those trips. He would always stop for gas and buy us both a candy bar.

I have some memories of my mother. Some of us kids were always hanging around the area and I was usually sitting in the dining room watching her. One day, I was depressed over some incident and she stopped whatever she was doing, came into the dining room and put me on her lap and consoled me.

I remember being in our parents' downstairs bedroom as they were getting dressed to go somewhere. My dad and mother walked around in the nude without thinking anything of it. I remember Mother preparing the noon meal in the kitchen. Dad would come home, kiss her hello and smack her on the butt with the newspaper.

When I was about 4½, my mother was ready to give birth and my dad told my sister Margaret and I to go into the bedroom where she was lying in bed. We were told to say goodbye to her because we wouldn't be seeing her again. We were kind of naïve at that age, so we went in and said goodbye to her. Two days later, we saw a hearse going out of the driveway, with her in it of course. And we didn't think to mourn at that age as we did not quite realize what had happened, but our lives were turned around.

At the time when my mother passed away, the mortgage on our house was due for foreclosure. My dad went down to Mr. Wilson at the bank. He was the bank's president and my dad discussed the situation with him. The bottom line was that Mr. Wilson extended the mortgage on Dad's word with a handshake.

I am one of 11 children; seven of us survived. Today, I am the only one of my family still living. My oldest sister was Eleanor Green and she lived to be around 21 or 22. She had tuberculosis and lived in the sanitarium in Orwell, New York. She died of a heart attack one night after having supper, as she climbed the stairs to her room.

Grandma Oot. (I am on her lap) L to R: Vincent, Gerald, Geraldine, Edith, Warren, Harold , Eleanor.

The second oldest was Vincent, and then there was Warren,

Gerald. Gerald had a twin sister, Geraldine, who passed away of scarlet fever at a young age. Then there was my sister Edith, myself, and my sister Margaret. There were several others after that, but I was too young to know them and can't remember their names.

After my mother died, life went on as it was. My dad had trouble getting someone to come in to take care of us, so my oldest sister, Eleanor, kind of took the place of my mother. She took care of us while she attended high school. She was extremely nervous, actually shaking at times, trying to get things done and keep it all together so we could get to school and all that.

My sister, Eleanor, at the Orwell Sanitarium.

Gertrude, my dad's second wife, was my first stepmother. My dad always said how my sister Edith reminded him more of our mother than the rest, and this got into Gertrude's craw, I guess, for some reason or another. She picked on Edith more.

One time, when our grandmother was living with us, she told Edith to "set the table and if you make one mistake, I'll send your brother Gerald out to get a switch and I'll switch you good." Well, Edith was trembling when she was setting the table and she made a mistake. Gerald got the switch and sure enough, Gertrude took Edith into the bathroom and started switching her until the switch broke. Then she started jabbing her with it in the legs. Wow. Well, my grandmother called my father, and he came home. Boy did he raise the roof with Gertrude. He said "Don't you ever touch her again." Edith was all bruised up from the stubby branch she used. Gertrude went kind of berserk with that.

One time, my sister Margaret and I were outside playing on the old Fordson tractor. Gertrude came out and said "You kids were told not to play on that tractor," even though there was nothing to get hurt on. My brothers and sisters were playing ball in the lot, on the other side of Mike Johnson's house, when Gertrude started switching my sister Margaret. I was kind of glad that she took Margaret first. In the meantime, my grandmother went out into the field to get my brother Vincent and he made her stop. Boy, she didn't like that at all. I was saved by the bell, more or less. That's the way things go.

When I was younger, we lived on West River Road. I used to have to do the gardening and all that stuff after school. I would come in in the evening to wash up in the laundry tub in the family room. One time, my stepmother, Winifred, was ragging at me for something, so I sassed her back and she clocked me on the back of my neck. As I keeled over I saw stars, but I recovered. Needless to say, I didn't sass her anymore that evening.

Gertrude eventually went off her rocker due to hardening of the arteries. She was placed in the mental institution in Marcy in Rome, New York, and eventually passed away there.

My second stepmother was named Winifred. Many years later, while in Sharon Center, Ohio, to visit our niece Ella, nephew Ken Raw, and her three brothers, we were visited by Karl and his daughter Katlin. We reminisced about Winifred. One summer, when we were younger, my father and Winifred took Ella and Beth Winn to the Goolie Club in the Adirondacks. (My dad belonged to the club.) Beth told us about her, Ella and Winifred being on the dock. Winifred spontaneously pushed Ella off the dock, knowing that she could not swim. Beth jumped in and saved her.

Ella Raw, and Beth Winn Guzzmann, Winifred's niece, came to visit at their house by Tannery Creek. Ella eventually went back home, but Beth Winn stayed on. When her parents came to pick her up, Winifred would purposely take her away so her parents couldn't take her back home. Finally, after the second time she did this, Beth's parents told her that if this happened again they were going to call the police. That took care of the problem.

The gals also told about how on their visits they had dolls in blankets and played outside while Winifred was cleaning. They looked inside and saw her in the nude. In the evening at suppertime, after Dad came home, the girls would have a glass of

13

milk with their meal. After they had one glass, they asked for a second. Winifred told them no, that one glass was enough. Dad told her to give the girls more milk, which she did reluctantly. At other times, at breakfast, we were allowed one cookie each, while at the same time she would sit there and feed her cocker spaniel several cookies.

Whenever Hans and Edith came to their house with the kids, Winifred would have a special itinerary which did not include the rest of the family. When she prepared meals for them, she would come up short on their food. Hans would always make the excuse that he had to get his car serviced and took the kids out, bought them a meal, came over to visit us and then go back to Dad's house.

While in Sharon Center, one of the brothers, Kris, told about an incident when he was younger and visiting my dad and Winfred. One morning during the visit, Kris got up in the morning to have breakfast. There was a bowl of oatmeal on the table and he assumed it was for him and he started eating it. The next thing he remembered was Winifred hitting him over the head with a broom and breaking it in two. She roared at him, saying it was her special mixture of oatmeal.

On one Thanksgiving at dinner, we were all gathered around the dining room table, our Aunt Margaret included. It was Dad's choice to serve us one person at a time. He finally finished serving all us nine people. Finally, his plate was the last one, he filled it, set it on his chair, turned around, sat on it briefly and set it quickly back up on the table. He apologized and we all had a good laugh. Then he went and changed his pants. We waited until he came back, said the blessing and all began to enjoy our meals while still discussing Dad's mishap in a fun way.

My dad had a bear rug with a bear's head on it that he had shot. It used to be on the cellar floor. One night, my sister Edith was having a 4-H club meeting on the side porch, and around sunset, the girls all started to go home. Gerald came up the side stairs with the bear rug and head on him and he groaned like a bear, scaring the dickens out of the girls. They all ran back into the house. He put it away and they went home afterwards. He thought it was a big joke.

During my dad's era, there was a belief that the oldest and the youngest sons would be most successful in their careers. Things did not always turn out that way. As it turned out, Vince being the oldest was the most successful, but the rest of us three boys did OK in spite of things. Wealth in life isn't always people who are successful.

Brother Gerald worked at the Victoria Mills after school and on weekends. He was allowed a portion of his pay to keep for himself. The rest was put in a fund set up by Winifred to pay our brother Vincent's tuition for college at Purdue University. In the meantime, Vincent also worked in the machine shop at the mill under machinist Percy Kitney until he went to school. Vincent was a very good student, so much so he didn't have to take final exams.

In the meantime, Gerald continued working and contributing to Vincent's fund. The idea was for Vincent to contribute to Gerald's college fund after he graduated and got a job. But, unfortunately, this did not happen. I remember seeing the tally book Winifred kept and the total was over $11,000 that Gerald had contributed. As it turned out, Gerald was able to attend Milwaukee School of Engineering for three years through an electrical course under the GI Bill of Rights for Veterans. He later finished his fourth year at Canton ATC and lived with my wife and me during that time.

My brother Vince was annoyed with me because of my favorite standing with my dad. He and I slept together in the same bedroom. There were four bedrooms for all of us to share. Warren and Gerald in one, Edith and Margaret in another and Eleanor was alone. (Dad had his drafting board in Eleanor's room and studied there for his professional engineering degree.) One night, I came upstairs to our room and found my flashlight had been crushed by Vince out of spite.

Another time, he and I were rearranging the beds in our room. I was in back of the metal headboard and Vince was at the base. For some reason, he pinned me between the headboard and the wall. I was at his mercy until he decided to release me. Fortunately, he did not harm me.

When he came home from college on recess, Vince would put boxing gloves on and spar with me. I held my own until my arms got so tired I couldn't hold them up to defend myself. He took the opportunity to pound on me. Each time he came home, we would have a go at it, with him winning out due to his size.

On one particular Christmas holiday, we were wrestling in the kitchen. We ended up on the floor and I happened to grab his hand, forcing it downward towards his wrist, which was a painful position. He started telling me to let loose, figuring I would, but I held it there and forced him to give up. When he got up, his face was beet red with humiliation over my first win over him.

Vince did not go into the service because his defective eye kept him from qualifying. Even though he was still superior in size and strength, my dad witnessed it all and chuckled. My relationship with Vince changed to a more mutual respect. One time, he and I went on a weeklong camping trip. We had a canoe, tent, food, and other necessary gear. I remember the downcast look on Dad's face as he said goodbye to us. I could only imagine what was going through his mind regarding our safety since he had already lost a child to drowning. As it was, we made it through the whole ordeal.

My two sisters, Edith and Margaret, each did a two-year course in a women's finishing school, Steven's College in Missouri. It was difficult for them to get in because of the school's high standards.

Edith ended up as an assistant buyer at Higbee's, a high-end department store in Cleveland. She eventually met her husband-to-be, Hans Laugesen, who worked for his dad's construction company, Hummel. Hans was a very skilled craftsman in carpentry and bricklaying. Eventually, he ended up owning the company and two of his older boys went to work for him. The third son, Karl, worked for a fuel company. I used to have weekly conversations with Hans, mostly about house repair, remodeling, etc.

Hans had a big old Lincoln Continental that he drove to Fulton with Edith for a visit. We would get together with Gerald and Betty and have a good family get together. If ever we had a family trauma, Edith would have Hans drive here for moral support. The only problem was the Lincoln would develop problems and require them to get help along the way. Whenever he got to Buffalo and this happened, I usually had a friendly customer that would help them out. Both of the two couples passed away, leaving a void in our lives.

My sister, Edith, and her husband, Hans.

Margaret ended up being a stewardess for Flying Tiger Airlines. It was there she met her husband-to-be, Hank, an airline navigator. He and others like him were put out of business by automation. They lived in Long Island before this and Hank would go on trips for two weeks at a time. They later moved to New Jersey. During the move they went through the Holland Tunnel, and after they got through, their canary was on its back asphyxiated by the fumes. He finally revived, but he couldn't sing for about a year.

Margaret and Hank lived in Pompton Lakes, New Jersey. I used to stay overnight at their house when I had to visit our factory in Linden, New Jersey. Eventually, after Hank lost his job, they bought a motor home, an Argosy Airstream trailer and moved west spending summers in Yellowstone at one of the lodges there. They had three boys that had grown up and moved on before all of that happened.

In the wintertime, Margaret and Hank would move on for the season to work at a place called Furnace Creek Ranch in Death Valley, California. They lived in a village with other people who worked at the ranch. There were also personnel that worked in the Borax mines. A lot of them spent their time getting drunk and quarrelsome.

One winter season, many years later, when my second wife, Sandy, and I were visiting her family in Bakersfield, we all drove over in her stepfather's motor home for a visit. We arrived in the afternoon and got settled in with Margaret and Hank. We ended up having dinner at the local village restaurant. We had a cocktail hour before dinner, and during this time we met a couple of college girls working there. We were chatting with them and found out they played the bongo drums for a local group. We asked them to play for us and they agreed to, after supper.

We met the girls after, in the lounge, and they had their bongos. But as it was, they froze and lost their confidence from being away from civilization for so long. After a while, I took the bongos and pretended to play them myself. There was one other teenage gal working there as a waitress. Margaret told us not to leave anything on our plates when we were through because the gal would take it to the kitchen and eat it. She was a German refugee who survived the bombing of Berlin and would eat any food available to survive. We lost all contact with them after Margaret passed away.

Left to right back: Me (age 16), Margaret, Warren, Vincent. Left to right front: Gerald, Winifred, Edith, Dad.

Chapter 2   Younger Years

When we lived on the West River Road, the house was set back in away from the road and we seemed to get a lot of rats from the river. My dad would give us 50 cents for every one we got in order to get rid of them.   We never got rid of all of them because they kept coming back.

One night, our dad had gone to bed and our brother Warren was down cellar waiting to catch one. He had a shotgun and shot the rat. My dad came flying out of bed down the stairs and my brother held up the rat and said "Well, you owe me 50 cents." My dad said, "50 cents, you're going to owe me more than that when you get through repairing the wall you just damaged.   What's the idea of blowing the gun off at night like that?" My brother came out the loser on that one.

Our back porch was up one story and we had a clothesline on a pulley that went out to a pole in the field. One day, I was up on the highway watching men digging a ditch for the highway. There was one fellow there that I was impressed with. He was from Chicago and worked in the stockyards. He wore a cowboy hat and

I was into Cowboys and Indians at that time, so I hung around with him. He chewed tobacco and he kept trying to get me to take some. I kept refusing him. One day I said "Oh, what the heck." I was too young to do it, but I took some and within two minutes my head started swirling around.

In the meantime, Winifred was up the road hollering at me. I was wondering how she knew what I had done, but I had to go home. Turns out, it wasn't that at all. What had happened was that the clothesline had broken and she was frustrated. So I helped get the clothes off and fixed the line. I was saved by the bell on that one.

We had special chores. My job was to mop the kitchen and laundry room floors. In the laundry, we had a bench on two sides where we used to eat our meals and on the other side of the kitchen was the dining room. I remember my sister used to sit there eating oatmeal. She didn't really like it. Unbeknownst to us, she was dumping it behind one of the benches against the wall. We found it when we pulled everything up to give the room a good cleaning. Anyway, we kind of laughed over that.

Every time I mopped those floors, Winifred would say I didn't do a very good job. She used to bawl me out. One Saturday, she was grocery shopping and my dad was home. I was really scrubbing those floors and my dad said I was doing a great job, and that made me feel good. Then Winifred came home from shopping, and said, "Well, you hardly cleaned these floors." She criticized me out of habit, I guess. My dad looked at me and we kind of shook our heads and took it where it was. Anyway, that's the way it was.

Dad got two chicken houses for me, set them out in our back lot and I proceeded to raise chickens. I bought about 100, all Rhode Island Reds. I raised them up beyond the boiler stage. Winifred talked my dad into making me sell them. For what reason I don't know, but I was very disappointed. I wanted to raise them to another stage (roasters) so they would be heavier and would bring in more money. But I sold them.

I still had Bantam chickens, roosters and other hens. The one rooster I had, my pet, used to jump up into the apple tree, which happened to be just outside my dad's bedroom window. Every morning at 4:00am he would start crowing and Dad was so mad about that. I went on vacation and when I came back he said "Come here, I want to show you something." He opened up the refrigerator door and showed me a cooked chicken upside down on a plate, and said "There's your pet rooster." I was very disappointed.

That surprised me because Dad had told me this story of his childhood when he had a pet hen: One Sunday, his family was having chicken and his father said, "You know what this chicken is?" and my father said "No." "It is your pet hen," he said. His father had cut the chicken's head off and cooked it up. My father said he couldn't eat chicken for a long time. That is why I was surprised he did the same thing to my rooster, but I could understand his reason wanting to get away from the noise, that crowing every morning. So what…

We really got some snow in those days and it would get colder. I remember one time it got down to 50 degrees below zero, believe it or not, and I was out on the road riding my bicycle. I didn't know any better at that age, it didn't faze me. We did not have snow blowers and such and my dad had us boys do all the shoveling by hand. Eventually all my brothers moved away for school, one thing or another and I became the sole snow shoveler.

On snowy winter days, I used to get up at 4 o'clock in the morning and worked until it was time to go to school. I usually shoveled our driveway and Porter Butts', our neighbor. When I got in school at Philips Street, I had trouble staying awake in class. The teacher nicknamed me 'Rip Van Winkle.'

My dad was very strict with me as far as shoveling the driveway. He made sure I kept the banks straight, aligned, with no jagged edges. Being an engineer, he wanted it done right. This lesson helped me later in life, in such projects as building a house.

In the summertime, we had other chores. As the days wore on, our stepmother Winifred would periodically step outside and call to us and make sure we were doing our jobs. She would say "Get to work."

I had the job of mowing the lawn by hand with a reel type mower. I was also given the job of mowing Porter Butts' lawn as part of my weekly ritual. We boys had to work eight hours a day outside. We would get up at four o'clock in the morning to get our time in weeding and tending the shrubs, and the big garden and we worked hard so we could get our time in by two o'clock and go play.

Sometimes we would go down to Indian Point, swimming in the Oswego River with other fellows in the neighborhood. We had a rope attached to a limb of a willow tree out in the water. We would take turns swinging on it over the water and drop off into the water.

We survived.

One summer, before I was ten years old, we were playing ball in our driveway, having a great time. I fell and landed on a cinder clinker and, unbeknownst to me, I cut the chords in my hand. My dad took me the doctor's and he somehow tied the chords together so I had the use of my hand. They have been OK ever since then and I am very thankful for that.

One summer when I was in my early teens, I was given the job of painting our house and we primed it with aluminum paint, the going thing at that time. So I got it all primed and then I put the outer coat on. I was up on the roof over the side porch and I spilled a can of paint. I got it before it was empty, but it ran down and we ended up with a silver roof.

My brother Gerald and I planted shrubs and had the whole place contoured off. One day, Gerald and I were in the shrubs weeding and I came upon a hop toad. There was some burdocks there and he took a burdock and threw one at the frog and he gulped it down. We couldn't believe it. So he gave him three or four more before we decided to stop it. We figured he would have a heck of a time with digesting them. It was kind of cruel of us to do that, but that was the way boys were, something to keep busy.

Dad decided to terrace the front lawn. We installed the shrubs and made a creek with a goldfish pond in the middle of it. It flowed back into a big holding tank installed in the cellar. It was then pumped back up to the head of the creek where it flowed back down again. Dad hoped that it would keep us busy.

During summers, we raised a big garden for food throughout the year. The garden required a lot of attention, keeping the weeds out, etc. In the fall, we dug up all the potatoes, put them in a pile, spreading them out to be washed, then dried and stored them in a bin down cellar. We pulled the carrots, topped them and stored them in a special bin of sand to preserve them. This cellar floor had stones on it instead of concrete. This allowed the vegetables and fruits to keep better from the moisture coming off the floor.

One summer, our septic system stopped working. It extended to the end of our back field. It was decided that the septic tank needed to be emptied. In those days, we didn't have septic people who'd come around and do pumping, so that's why we had to do it ourselves. Gerald and I were given the job. We dug down to the opening, removed the door and an ugly strong smell was emitted. We had no choice but to dip the sewage out one bucket at a time. We then spread it out on the open fields.

As the contents got lower we had to put a ladder down in the tank and climb down to reach the contents. We would take turns dipping it out and handing it out to the one on top to dispose of it. Gerald volunteered to go down first. As he started in, he handed the first bucketful to me and explained, "This one is for you and the next one is for me." This procedure was continued for the whole process, putting some humor into this seemingly unbearable chore. We managed to lighten up our attitude towards it and before we knew it, the job was done.

One summer, Dad decided to build a foundation for a two-car garage attached to the north side of the house. He also decided to install a large turntable out of the garage floor so that when he drove into the garage, he could turn the car around and face the outside entrance, thus not having to back out and turn the normal way. A nice idea. He installed several cement posts in the flooring to support it for the turn. Unfortunately, this was never completed while we lived there.

Between our house and Porter Butts' in the back side porch we were on a hill that went straight down. On Porter Butts' side there was a cement stone wall, and the shrubs grew up so you could hardly see the wall. My dad had these two Purple Martin houses – Martins are birds that like insects – on corner of each side of the house, near the shrubs. Cats would come over and wait for the birds. When the Martins would push their young out of the nest, the cats would get them.

Dad hated cats. One time, we were sitting on the sun porch in front of the house and looked up toward Porter's house and saw that the window was broken. We didn't know why, but come to find out, Warren was sitting out back and saw the cat on the cement wall and he shot his 12-gauge. The bullet went through the corner of our porch and over toward Johnson's house, but apparently it had played itself out by then. When my dad found out, boy was he mad. "Who did this?" he asked. Warren said, "Bob did it." But my dad knew better, and Warren finally admitted it. He gave him the dickens, anyway. He got the 106th; the end of that story. That's the way things happen.

We had one neighbor at our grandfather's house who rented there and they had a bulldog. He was a friendly dog who liked to play around. We were all gathered around outside, just talking, having a good time. My brother Warren got the dog chasing him and the next thing I knew, he jumped up and bit Warren right in the rear end. It was the funniest thing. The dog didn't do it viciously, but Warren asked for it. That was the end of that escapade.

When we lived on West River Road, Porter Butts, a shoe salesman, and his wife lived on the side toward the city. Mr. Butts was very good to us children. He would take us around the 4th of July to buy us fireworks. He liked my brother, Warren, and would send him in to buy the fireworks. When Warren came out, Porter would give him more money and send him back in for more. (He did this about four times.) We got the biggest kick out of that. He didn't have children of his own.

On the other side lived Mike Johnson; he worked for my father at the paper mill. He fired the boilers there. He did extra work for people after he finished his job at the mill. He would do lawns in the summer and shovel snow in the winter. I remember him bringing his lunch in a market basket containing several sandwiches. Mike was a big muscular man with a big appetite. In the wintertime, he would play in the snow with us, making snowmen, forts, having snowball fights and sledding down the hill. He would also very carefully tow us on our sleds with his Model A Ford.

Growing up, we lived across the road from Fred Desmond's farm. Mr. Desmond lived by himself. He had a buggy that he kept in a shed attached to the barn. He had some chickens and I remember he slaughtered his own pigs. It was terrible. You would hear them squeal when he went to work on them. I remember my dad would buy half a pig from him. He would get it butchered and pack it away for our consumption later on.

Mr. Desmond had a horse that lived to be 32 years old. The horse was kept in the barn and out in the pasture. My sister Margaret and I used to get on a telephone pole stump and jump onto its back for a ride. He was quite a horse. I remember falling off one time and landed on one of those darn telephone pole stumps on my hip, but I survived.

Mr. Desmond also raised English setters. Most every night, his female brood dog would come over to our back porch door and my dad always had a treat for her. One day after she had a brood of puppies, she brought one over to our house and left it there on our front porch step. My brother and sister found it there and took it back home. My dad planned on visiting Mr. Desmond's to purchase one of the pups for hunting. He went over that night and actually picked out the same pup the mother had brought over earlier that day. I guess the mother wanted us to have it in the beginning. By the way, they named the dog Della, short for armadillo, I guess. It seemed to fit the dog.

Eventually, we got another English setter named Ted. We kept him out back with Della. He became a very good pet of mine. One day, we had him out back and he was barking. There was an infestation of fleas. He walked out to the path and you could hear him jumping. So we got him out of there and treated him. He got over that. Another instance, my dad caught a snapping turtle and he had it in a bushel basket out back where he was going to butcher it to eat, I guess. I saw Ted with his head over the basket sniffing the turtle. The turtle was ready to snap at his nose. That would have been a bad one, and I pulled Ted out of there. We saved him there.

Mr. Desmond used to sit in one of his out buildings smoking his pipe and napped while in his old rocking chair. He had a stove in this building for heat so this was a place where he relaxed. Mr. Desmond passed away quietly, sitting on his rocking chair in that shed.

The Hillicks ended up with Mr. Desmond's farm. This is how I came to raise chickens. Mrs. Hillick hired me to clean out the chicken coops and various other jobs for 29 cents an hour. I also helped Bob Pooler, a friend, slaughter and clean chickens to get them ready for market.

In the summertime, I used to work at this farm down the road owned by Malford Levee. He was an electrician who worked for my dad and he farmed on the side. He did haying by hand. We had to cut the hay and then put it on the wagon and move it to the hay loft. Boy, it was really hot up there in July, when we were usually doing it. At noontime, his wife would cook a country meal: canned beef, gravy, potatoes and vegetables. Boy, did I look forward to that.

I didn't mind working on Malford's farm, even though one time he hollered at me. What happened, he got caught underneath the rake and he was afraid the horses would bolt. So he had me hold onto them until he got out from under them. Fortunately, he did not get hurt there.

Mrs. Levee always had a litter of kittens. I'd be sitting in the kitchen and they would be hanging on the drapes or somewhere in the room and she would go after them because they would pull the strings out of them. And Malford always had his pet cat that he kept in his lap by the stove. He had an old wood-burning kitchen stove, which were familiar in those days. And usually each kitchen had a clock that tic toc-ed, otherwise a comforting feeling.

Malford knew a lot of poems and he would recite them all morning while we were working. I don't know how he could remember all those poems, but he was very entertaining, and he was good to me. His wife was our first teacher. At school, there was a superintendent who came around from time to time. His name was Mr. Gardner and he would check on each school to see how things were going. He would come in and want to know if any of the kids had been bad. Mrs. Levee would tell him who was bad, so he would go grab the kid, pick him up right in front of everyone and give him the dickens, scaring the heck right out of the kid. Then he would set him down. He never laid a hand on us other than that. We always looked forward to him from that standpoint.

We were raised on raw milk. The Pooler's farm, which was on West River Road, had cows and we got raw milk. Grandmother Pooler would come down Saturday, looking for her check for the milk. She came in with a horse and buggy, all set to go downtown. One time, we didn't have the money in time and she was very disappointed, but she trusted us.

Another incident was when my brother Gerald and I were visiting our neighbor lady. She made the greatest lemon meringue pie and was just a real nice person. Eventually, she became Gerald's mother-in-law when he married her daughter. For some reason or other, my stepmother resented her and told us we were to never go over there to visit. When she happened to catch us over there, she came in through their garage door and started up the stairs. I ran down the stairs faster, and as I did, she grabbed me by the back of my shirt and ripped it off. I kept right on going and went up to another neighbor's to hangout until she cooled off.

In the meantime, she went up to Syracuse where my dad was at a meeting and told him the works. My brother Gerald and I slept in the same bed up in one of the bedrooms and that night here comes my dad. He turns the light on and says "What's going on here?" He gave me the dickens about doing all that. As a result of all that, he announced that I would go out to the country to Grant's farm at Bowens Corners for the summer. It suited me fine because I got out there.

On the farm we used to get up at 4:00 o'clock in the morning and do chores in the barn. Then we would come in to a tremendous country breakfast. Boy was that good. I used to run the old John

Deere tractor, cultivating, and we did the haying and things like that. We were the last ones in the neighborhood doing the haying. In the afternoons, Mrs. Grant would come out with a chocolate cake and some nice cold milk around 4 o'clock and that recharged our batteries so we were able to get the work done.

In the fall when it was time for me to go back to school, my dad said I had to come home. The Grants wanted me to stay over and that was fine with me. Dad made me come home and get back to school. I guess that was the best thing in the end.

The Bock family, Carl, Frank, and Genevieve, attended my school, District #17, too. Their mother would bake large loaves of Polish bread once a week. We always found out when and made a point to accompany Frank home. We would end up getting a slice of this delicious bread.

Mrs. Cusac lived across the lot from our house. Her husband was partially blind and he had strings set up around the backyard so he could get around. He could see just a little bit. I remember one time I saw him out behind our house way beyond my chicken coup. I walked down there and asked him what he was doing down there heading toward the river and he said he was trying to find his way home. I told him he was way off his route and escorted him home, which he was very glad about.

Mr. Cusac didn't have any children, of course, so he had to take the ashes from the coal out by himself. He saved the good coal so he could use it over again.

He had a building out back, which was an old railroad car. He let me use it and I raised chickens in there. We used to play up in his barn and we liked to play there because there was nothing there, it was deserted.

Mrs. Cusac used to come over to our house and help out when we didn't have a mother or stepmother. She helped with doing dishes and baking, taking care of us kids in general, she was a very nice lady. We were blessed to have them as neighbors.

In back of the Cusac's field, towards the river, there was an old gravel bed. I remember we used to go there and pick wild strawberries, enough to make strawberry shortcake. They were small, but boy were they good. I really enjoyed them. In the summer I always remember strawberry season. We'd make a big plate of shortcake and strawberries for supper and that was all we had. It was really delicious. After my brother Warren moved away from town, that's all he complained about: not getting strawberries. So whenever he came to town for a visit, if it was strawberry season, we made sure we had strawberry shortcake for him.

There was another gravel bed over by what they called Indian Point where the waste recycling is now. It used to be Brennan's farm across the road from us. There was a big hill there and we used to go up to the top and find Indian arrowheads. We used to ski down it in wintertime. I remember Bob Pooler and my brother had a jitney Model B Ford they'd stripped down. They used to drive it all over and I remember they would drive it up that hill and come back down, it was quite a challenge to get there. It was a rear-wheel drive of course, a nice old buggy.

I have a picture of that with him behind the wheel. My brother, Gerald, was there and Bob Pooler, Bill Erb, and myself. My dad would take moving pictures of us on his 8mm camera. Unfortunately, they got destroyed by mildew being stored in the fruit cellar. All of those years of filming our childhood activities were gone. Before that, my dad would show some of them on Saturday night, then ended up with showing a cartoon.

Another fellow lived across from the Poolers, Brian Matthews. He was the same age as Gerald; they went to school together. I remember going downtown with him one time and we jogged home from the city limits. He encouraged me to keep going until I was out of breath. He taught me to get into running and build up my endurance that way.

One day, on the way home after school, my sister Margaret and I stopped at Tannery Creek and went down the bank near the water to look at a dead skunk laying there. We looked it over and poked at it with sticks and we eventually went on home. After we got home and went into the house someone let out a yell and told us to go back outdoors as we wreaked of skunk odor! We had to change clothes, take a bath and whatever else that was necessary to get rid of that odor. A lesson learned!

One winter day, when we were older, two friends and I decided to ski across the Oswego River to visit the Roger's farm. After we started out and got into the center of the river, the ice started to sag under our weight. We had no choice but to go as fast as we could to get safely to the other shore. I don't know if I was more afraid of Dad finding out or breaking through the ice. If we did, we would have been swept under the current. The next dumber thing we did was to ski back across in another location. We should've bummed a ride or walked back home. But we made it!

Another late winter day, March 31, when I was a young teenager, Bob and Don Clemmons and I decided to shoot the rapids in Tannery Creek. We had an Old Town canoe stored upside down on the ground and we chopped it free from the ice. We put it in at the bridge on Honey Hill Road and proceeded down the creek, which was actually flooded. We were moving along pretty good until we ran into a submerged barbed wire fence across the creek. I was in the bow and each time we tried to free ourselves, we would take on water. The only thing I felt we could do was jump onto the bank, which I did.

I turned around and saw Bob and Don in the water being held by the current against the wire. This saved them from being washed down the stream. I was able to pull them out safely onto the bank. We were soaked through like drowned rats. I took my boots off, drained them and proceeded to run over a half mile in my stocking feet in the snow to our friend Erb's home. We dried out, got warm and walked home.

The next day, we went back to the creek to find out what happened to the canoe. We found that it had pushed under the submerged wire and traveled down the creek, hitting an island sideways and partially breaking it in two. We were able to break it free, took it home, the intending to put it back together. This never happened and it was thrown into the trash. That canoe today, restored, would be worth over $3,000.

We would go to the Saturday night square dances around our area. Vincent and his buddies used to hang out at the dances. Vince was a pretty good boxer. His two friends would pick a fight with someone on the floor and Vince would go outside and duke it out with them. I remember our group of younger boys would be dancing a set and guys would all pick up the gals in the air, showing off our strength. We'd twirl them around to the music with them all squealing.

Bob Pooler used to work at the Roger's Dairy across the river. In order to get there, he would swim across the river in the nude with his clothes on a plank to transport them and keep them dry. He always used to tell us about this guy, Lelan, and his terrific build. Finally, we got to go over and meet him. He was quite a specimen. He worked out with weights and we learned that he wrestled for

SU where he went to school. He ended up being the NYS Junior Wrestling champion. He used to demonstrate his strength to us by going into a handstand and doing pushups on them. We were in awe.

Lelan had a younger brother, Lorry, who worked in the milk house (processing, bottling). Both boys would deliver milk to their customers around the area. After delivering was over, Lorry would run the milk house and Lelan would sit in the house counting the money from the route. While doing this, Lelan would recognize the valuable coins and ended up becoming a very well-off coin collector. Later during the day, they would help their father with the farm chores such as haying, etc. During the war, gas was rationed and we would go over to Mrs. Rogers to bum some gas ration tickets and she gave us a few.

I remember when I was around 13 years old, after school we went to someone's house and they had barbells there. The first I had ever seen them. They were showing me different lifts, so I tried doing a military press. That is to stand up and push the weight over your head. The first time I did it, I was able to lift 75 pounds, which is pretty good for my age and all that stuff. So from then on it was bodybuilding.

I used to work out in my cellar and our family room, we had weights there. We also worked out in Bob Pooler's barn, we had weights set up in there. We even worked out in wintertime, in cold weather. One time there was four or five of us together and we thought what the heck and we would do this in the nude and it was colder than hell in the wintertime. So we worked out that session in the nude, but fortunately we didn't get sick.

Later on, during one of my semesters at the College of Forestry, I used to work out at the Syracuse University gym and other body building programs they offered. One was with the parallel bars, where I worked up to mounting the bars, swinging into a handstand, dropping down on a shoulder roll and dismounting. I also worked out on the high bars and the rings. One other feat that I accomplished, after building up strength and coordination, was to sit on the gym floor with my feet out in front of me, raise my feet up under me and back up into a handstand. I'd then do a dozen pushups while in the handstand. I first saw this done by Lelan Rogers when he was attending SU. He was also the New York State Junior Wrestling Champ.

I was also able to do a handstand and walk the length of the gym floor on my hands. These accomplishments were all quite a contrast to the results of my studies. At one time while working out, I was invited by the SU wrestling coach to be on their team, but I declined.

When I was younger, we lived on the west side and we used to go over across the river to Ed Bellinger's house on the east side. Lee Pooler and he were good buddies. They were good mechanics and always working on cars and doing them over. And I learned how to file the caps on the piston rods on an old Chevy I had and take up the tension. We would take all the shims out so that was a step to keep the thing running.

Top photo: Me and Lee Pooler. Right photo: Me, Fran Parsons, Ed Bellinger.

I used to hang out with Ed a lot, and he would take me for a ride in his car in the wintertime and boy he was quite a driver. I never saw anyone get into a car, a strange car, and parallel park like it was nothing. He used to go like crazy even on the icy roads. I remember we were going down Honey Hill one winter and, in order to see, he put his thumb on the frosted-up windshield to make a peephole. He used to scare the dickens out of me, but he was a good guy. He really knew his automobiles. Lee Pooler could take an old truck, tear it all down and put it back together, almost like new. He was a good mechanic also.

On one Sunday, Ed, Lee and some of the other guys came over. I was in the throes of filing the caps on my car. They wanted to get ready to go, just to go someplace, so Ed proceeded to file the caps down some. He filed them down tighter than the dickens. Too much, so we had an awful time getting the thing to turn over. We ended up with a crank on the front end that someone had to jump up and down on it. We tried pulling it with another car and it finally broke loose. We were OK....crazy things, I got a big kick out of that.

On one of our dance nights out I met a gal near Phoenix that I thought was pretty nice and we became a number. I would go out to pick her up in my dad's '98 Olds and take her to the dances. I was really enthralled with her to the point she was the only girl for me. Her older sister disagreed and did everything she could to break us up. Eventually, my girlfriend tired of me. I ended up getting a Dear John letter from her when I was in the service in Pearl Harbor. I was crushed by this, but had to accept it and respected her being honest. I never got over this.

Back in those days, there was a lot of prejudice going on, particularly against the less fortunate people who migrated here and held menial jobs. As it turned out, these people were very resourceful and hardworking individuals who ended up being well off, to their credit. I remember Winifred asking me if my girlfriend was Jewish, based on her last name (which I am respectfully omitting). I told her that I did not know and I asked her what the difference was.

Chapter 3   School

My first seven years were at District #17 country school. It closed and I did 8th grade at the Phillip Street School in Fulton. Every morning as school started, we would all stand up say the Lord's Prayer, pledge allegiance to the flag and sing 'My Country Tis of Thee." We would find ways to have fun on our breaks and lunch time. We had teeter totters and swings, another was to toss a tennis ball over the roof shouting "halley, halley over" to a partner on the other side to catch it and toss it back using the same method.

Our school was right on the west edge of the golf course where we played baseball. We'd also play Cowboys and Indians in the pine trees on the east side of the school grounds. In the wintertime, we would go out on the golf course and slide down on our bottoms. I got the bright idea to tear a Coca Cola sign off the clubhouse and use it for a toboggan. It worked fine until I got home and my dad chewed me out for taking the sign.

My brother Gerald was a prankster. One day at the country school, after a rain and on our break, somehow everyone started to call me 'elephant ears' and Gerald just egged them all on, making me more furious. I was running after each one of them and trying to catch them and shut them up. This just kept getting worse until, finally, Gerald picked up an empty burlap sack that was soaked with muddy water and wrapped it around my head, making me madder yet.

At this point, recess was over and the teacher made me go to the back of the school into the woodshed. She locked me in to cool me down. This made me more infuriated and I picked up a chunk of wood and threw it at the door. Just as I was about to throw a second chunk of wood, the teacher slowly opened the door and calmly said to me, 'You wouldn't throw that at me, Bob?" All of a sudden, this seemed to calm me down. She came into the room and had a sympathetic talk with me. Eventually, I really calmed down and I went back into the classroom and nothing more came of it.

Another morning, before we were called into class, one of the students, Junior Reno, who was from a broken home, started to antagonize Gerald. Gerald would chase him all over the yard. Junior made it up a large maple tree where Gerald couldn't reach him. Junior continued to antagonize Gerald from the tree. Gerald started climbing the tree to get at him. Junior ended up urinating on Gerald. Just then, the bell rang for all to come to classes. Of course, Gerald had to go into the boy's room and clean himself up as best he could.

Another time in class, Garold Gibbons sat behind me. We were exchanging comments and I turned back around. All of sudden, he jabbed at the side of my head with a lead pencil, hitting the inside of my ear. Fortunately, it did not hit the ear drum. I do not remember what kind of punishment the teacher gave him, other than a good scolding.

One morning recess in winter, everyone got dressed to go out to play in the snow. I got dressed also and was looking for my hip boots I wore to school and couldn't find them. Everyone looked all over. Suddenly, one of the boys found them in the boy's room chemical toilet. We fished them out, cleaned them out and hung them in the wood shed to dry out so I could wear them home after school. Eventually, it was found out that Junior admitted to throwing them in the toilet. Here again, I am not sure how he was reprimanded.

One day after school in the wintertime, we were walking home with the two Clement boys, who lived on a poultry farm by the river. Their names were Bob and Don. We decided to explore the swampy river edge. Bob and I walked out on the black ice and all of a sudden the ice broke under my left leg, letting me down into the water up to my hip. Just then, Don started running back up the bank shouting "Help, help, I'm drowning!" Bob was standing beside him and said, "You are not the one in the water" and told him to go get the rope, which he did. They pulled me out and I had to walk home in wet pants.

Chapter 4   Growing Up and Going in the Navy

I worked at the two paper mills (Victoria & North End) assisting three or four millwrights. I couldn't help but to marvel at their intuition working through several different seemingly impossible problems. Just when everyone was ready to give up, usually Les Marley, the welder, would say, "Now just a minute," and within a short time, he or another millwright would come up with a solution. Those experiences were a good lesson in life, in more ways than one.

My high school graduation picture.

On school days, I worked the 4pm-10pm shift at the North End

Paper Mill doing maintenance repair. On holidays and weekends we worked on the boilers and other machines that needed repair. I was assistant to Les Marley, a welder. He did acetylene and arc welding. He also did steam pipe repair and installations.

One of the maintenance jobs we had at the North End Paper Mill was to replace all of the old sprinkler heads in the ceilings, which were at least 24 feet high. We tied two 24-foot extension ladders together at their tops and spread the feet out on the floor, making them stable. Two of us would climb the ladders, one on each side to reach the sprinkler heads in the ceiling. We carried a 24-inch pipe wrench with a piece of pipe called a come-a-long to place over the pipe handle, which gave us more leverage to turn the sprinkler heads and remove them. As we removed the heads, there was an awful odor that escaped from the sprinkler's pipe.

We would attach the new head and go down the ladder and set up at the next station. This was a very dangerous job because of the instability of the set up and the height. Fortunately, we respected that and remained safe during all the installations. Another job we had was covering all the steam pipes with asbestos and covering the outside of the covers with shellac. The asbestos was the insulation in the covers.

We usually worked on the maintenance of the boiler on a hot July day. I would get inside the water jacket on top of the boiler and chip away all the slag buildup on the walls from heat and hard water. I usually worked with my shirt off and sweat a lot. I was covered with dust by the end of the day and welcomed a shower.

One day when I was younger, my dad came home from working at the North End running a high voltage power line. He was in terrible pain from the shock he encountered from the line. It took a long time for the pain to subside. He was lucky he wasn't electrocuted; that would have been a terrible loss to our family.

My dad was always good to me and let me use his 1941 Oldsmobile. I remember back when I was still in high school and I first obtained my driver's license, my dad let me take his Olds and I burned up a tank of gas just going around the Dizzy Block that night. I was very thrilled to be driving and had to show off my feelings.

That Olds had one of the first hydrostatic transmissions. As luck would have it, the car started slipping the way a clutch would wear out. One particular night, I coasted home and parked it on our front lawn. Fortunately, the Oldsmobile Company fixed it because of it being an innovation and having some flaws that needed to be worked out. This was a relief to me. I felt guilty because it happened while I was driving it. At times, it seemed that every time I used the car, something would go wrong while on a date. The tire would go flat, etc.

After I graduated from high school, my dad wanted me to go on to college. He said all of us boys, all of his children, should have a college education. I attended Syracuse University School of Forestry until I got a call from the draft board and had to report. Before that, when the war broke out, I had asked my brother's future father-in-law, "Will I have to go?" And he said "No, it'll be over before that happens." But I got a notice in the mail saying I was drafted. They were always kidding about getting a special letter from Uncle Sam. I was deferred for a while because I was in my first year at the School of Forestry. I was 18.

My dad had a lot to do with me being in the Navy. He thought that was a safer place to be. He had some friends, made some calls and pulled some strings. Normally, prior to showing up that day, you wouldn't know where you're going. As you were in line, they'd tell you where to go because they had to fill certain allotments.

I ended up in Sampson doing my ten weeks there, near Geneva, New York, on the Finger Lakes. Most of the guys there were from Central New York. That was funny because all the guys at Christmastime thought for sure that they would let us go home to spend Christmas. Don't know why we had to stay there, but they wouldn't let us off the base. Some of the guys were crying they were so homesick. But we got through it.

It sure was cold over there; it was in January or February. You'd see cracks in the walls through the siding. I had all my clothes on, my pea coat, in order to keep warm. We used to have to march as part of the training. The first week, our feet were freezing, but we had to keep right on going. The next week, my feet were accustomed to it. It is amazing how your body gets used to something.

I remember we had one week of KP duty, kitchen police. We had to clean up the mess hall and we had to mop the floors once a day. I thought I would be clever and I used two mops because I was strong enough and I got all done and the chief said "Do it over." Even though it was clean, I had to do it over. Of course, that was the idea, getting you to behave, respond to the leaders. Some young guys were a little cocky and officers would belittle them to get them down to the right level. You had to respect authority. They wanted us to act as a unit and respond to instructions.

But I had had chores that helped me prepare for the service. Twice a week, I had to mop the floors, mop the cellar stairs and things like that. I made four loaves of bread a week. I had to shovel all the snow around the fire hydrants. We had a garden, so I was busy all the time. Eight hours a day I had to work. So, I learned discipline from a young age.

We had to do ten weeks of training and we had one night, one afternoon actually, of liberty. We went into Geneva, and had pretty good time. We met some girls and hung around with them and we had to be back by seven or eight o'clock, I guess. I remember one time we went into the PX and I bought ten Nestlé candy bars. I ate them all, boy I just craved them. They didn't make me sick, though. That was the extent of it.

After I left boot camp, I was shipped to Detroit Naval base to take up becoming an electrician for the Navy. I remember the ride out on the train. It was raining, it was evening. I ended up in the Buffalo train station and we had to sleep sitting up in our seats. In the morning we went on to Detroit, where we did the classes at their Naval base. While at the Detroit Armory, we were given weekend passes, allowing us to go home by rail. One chief wouldn't release us until a couple hours later, making it difficult to catch our train. A good friend, Bob Pooler, attended the Detroit school a year earlier and met a local gal. Bob Pooler's mother kept in contact with the girl and invited her to come to Fulton for a visit and asked me to bring her home, which I did.

Next, I was shipped to Treasure Island in San Francisco by rail. We had bunks on the train, but had a problem of soot coming in from the two engines pulling us. We couldn't shower and food was obtained at stops in lunch boxes. It was a very boring ride. I've forgotten how many days it took to get out there, but I was standing out there between the cars kind of taking in the scenery and one of the officers came over and said "Hey, you're not supposed to be out here." Then he went back in. I guess he was afraid I was going to jump ship.

As we arrived in California, the weather was extremely hot and muggy. I stayed there about two to three weeks not doing much. I worked out and had liberty, but did not go out too much. We rode the cable cars and it was a novelty going up the steep hills.

We were loaded aboard a troop ship named Zoella-Lykes, a reconverted Merchant Marine cargo ship. There were about 1,500 sailors on the front of the ship and 70 officers on the back of the ship. They had better things than we had. We all got seasick, pretty much, on the way over. I was doing OK until my friend told me to not to think about it. Well, he kept talking about it so much that one day I'm going up stairs on a drill and I had to throw up. So I threw up in my hat and cleaned it up afterwards. Then I went up on deck to do drill. Everybody was getting sick. It was a few days before we seemed to get over it.

We broke down and ended up in Pearl Harbor for three weeks. I remember coming into Hawaii, you could see the islands in the distance. The islands looked like a green pencil line across the horizon, a brilliant green. They got bigger and bigger as we sailed into the harbor where we saw a lot of devastation. There were still the results of the bombing.

We had to have repairs done to the ship and we were there for two weeks. We looked for things to do, so we swam in the pool. One evening, we went into Hawaii. (I've forgotten which island we were on.) We had a nice time and had to be back in not too late a period. We were moored against another ship. A lot of the sailors were into the shore. The other ship was tied onto us and the sailors from the other ship boarded our ship and went down below deck and raised the dickens. Finally, they went back on their own ship.

We were allowed one night liberty in Honolulu. We worked out and swam in the base pool. We enjoyed fresh pineapple and a lot of other fruits. It was quite a sight to see the devastation from the Japanese attack. Actually, the war with Japan ended while we were there "VJ Day." I heard about the war ending in the evening. I was in the exercise area when an officer said it was over. Then the cheering started and the rockets went off. We were sure, we didn't doubt it.

I was taking the somber note of what had happened and who we lost. Of course, the sad part for all of us was that we still had to go on to relieve sailors who had been stationed, as we were occupational troops.

We landed in Samar, Lyte Golf, in the Philippines and were assigned to a ship repair base called Manicani. There were several floating dry docks used for ship repair. They sat idle, as the war was over. There were good naval personnel assigned there and I ended up as a master of arms at the mess hall. I was stationed at one of two entrances to maintain order.

I made friends while I was there, but they didn't last. We said we were all going to keep in touch, but that fades away. However, Jack Durfey was one lifelong friend from the service. I didn't know him until it was time to muster out (Editor's note: "Muster out" or "mustering out" refers to being discharged from service.). We all ended up in this village and there he was. He ended up on the ship to go home before I was and I was madder than hell. I called him for some of the information and that resulted in a lifelong friendship. We ended up being neighbors.

While off duty, we worked out with weights, ran and did some boxing. I had a good buddy, smaller than me, and we liked to spar around in the boxing ring. One day, a fellow my size showed up and wanted some exhibition fights for the troop entertainment. I ended up reluctantly participating and ended up facing the fellow who was so eager to get in the ring with me because, previously, I ended up beating him. The write-up in our troop paper stated that I had passed up many opportunities for a knock out.

That was quite an experience. I definitely did not want to pursue that sport. It was extremely hot and muggy and I developed "prickly heat," which was sort of like shingles. There didn't seem to be a cure for it. We played basketball in the hot sun and would lose anywhere from three to five pounds of body weight.

My job as a master of arms in the mess hall afforded me extra good food and plenty of it. A master of arms is like a police officer.

There were 6,000 people going through there each meal and I would be up at the end of one of the entrances maintaining order in the lines. It went good, I didn't get any backlash. They had to respect me.

We experienced tiny bugs in our bread. You could always tell a new recruit by the way he would hold the slices of bread up to the light and tried picking the bugs out. The old timers didn't bother. We experienced heavy torrential rains that actually flash flooded the mess hall for a short time. After it was over and the water subsided, it left a large land crab on the floor.

On the trip from Hawaii to the Philippines, we ran into some foul weather. There was a lot of sea sickness causing diarrhea and vomiting. The latrine was in the bow area, running from one side to the other. As the ship rolled side to side the residue in the latrine would also move from side to side. Needless to say, it was a bad time for the sailor who had to stick his head down there to vomit.

Once, after one of our main meals of chili, I wandered out back outside of the kitchen where the garbage accumulated and there were five or six Filipinos standing around the waste cans dipping into the discarded left-over chili with pieces of bread and eating it as if it were a gourmet meal. These people were very poor and got food wherever they could. No one tried to stop them.

One day, we had duty cleaning out a caged-in area of outdated food. There were Filipinos outside begging us to throw some over the fence to them, which we were not supposed to do. We did throw some of the canned food to them when no one was looking. This showed us how poor and desperate they were for food. Every night, we had an exhibition match and movies afterward – outside. We watched as the personnel came in and took their seats. One sailor, an old timer having been there for four years, took a shine to a Filipino girl and wound up bringing her and her mother to the show. One particular night, they came in with him trailing behind. He was trying to make up after a spat. The troops got a kick out of this and gave him the raspberries. They eventually took their seats and calmed down.

One night, a group came in with a monkey attached to one of the sailors. Part of the group stayed back holding the monkey, while the rest including the owner went into the crowd and took their seats. The rest of the group let the monkey loose and it went right over to its owner. Later on, with the movie going we could see the monkey on his owner's head, watching the show.

One incident I remember from the Philippines was this: I came around a corner and there was a young girl in a tub of water with her clothes on taking a bath, using a pail to pour water over herself. She was grinning from ear to ear. That's how they took a bath. I thought that was quite the thing.

We were transferred to a base in Samar for the trip back to the states. It was one of the liberty ships built by Kaiser. On the way back we ran into heavy seas which caused the ships bow to raise forty feet out of the water and drop back down with a tremendous force causing vibration through the ship but fortunately it held together.

Every sailor felt a huge sense of pride and relief as we passed under the Golden Gate Bridge. We were back home in the U.S.

Me, left, and my brothers, Gerald (top) and Warren (middle).

When I first arrived in 'Frisco, I called home and of all people to answer the phone, I got Winifred. Her comment was, "Oh, are you back." It did not give me a warm and fuzzy feeling. Some of us were shipped south of San Francisco to Vallejo, a naval base there. I was assigned to a sea-going tug that was used to tow decommissioned ships to a graveyard several miles inland. It was quite a sight to see all of those ships at anchor. One time, we were towing a submarine and we went aboard out of curiosity. As soon as I went down inside, I became claustrophobic and couldn't get out of there fast enough.

I was finally discharged at Vallejo with mustering out pay. I was in the service for a two-year stint, but was mustered out after 19 months and a few days because the war was over. At that time, we were reenrolled back in the Navy for four years on an inactive status. This gave us special status in case we had to be called back up in a national emergency. The bus trip back home was very uncomfortable as we were on it around the clock. We slept in seats that reclined. We made occasional stops at mealtime long enough to get food, etc. The busses west of the Mississippi were very uncomfortable. Beyond that, we were transported in more modern and comfortable ones.

On the first leg of our trip, the driver picked up a couple of inebriated cowboys and he had to send them off the bus for being uncontrollably rowdy. On one stop in Des Moines, Iowa, I found the people very friendly and easy going. I was always sorry that I

59

didn't stay over for a few days, but I was too anxious to get back home. As we arrived in Cleveland to change buses I was becoming very uncomfortable and nauseated from the continuous riding.

I met a friendly gentleman who I struck up a conversation with. I told him how I was feeling and wished I could stop somewhere for a bath and rest. He knew just the place. It was a YMCA in Buffalo. We ended up stopping there and getting separate rooms. We did the steam bath in the nude. And he ended up following me back to my room and laying on my bed and not in a hurry to leave. Our rooms were open ceilings partitions.

All of a sudden there was a knock on my door, and a gentleman entered, stating, "Did I hear someone say Oswego, New York?" We found out that he was from there. We talked a while and my friend got off my bed and they all left. I finally got to bed and slept until 4 am. I got up, dressed, and left for the bus station to take me home.

I arrived back home to Fulton midmorning and went directly to the Victoria Paper Mill to meet up with my dad. He was overwhelmed seeing me and how I had changed physically. He was very proud of me and introduced me to all the mill personnel almost to the point of embarrassment. That was okay. After all his losses: our own mother, then Gertrude and four of his children all died. I knew he loved me.

When I got back, my friends didn't treat me any different. Going in the service for those 19 months matured me and made me look at things differently. While I was in, I took a course on writing and one on supervision, and that kind of matured me.

When I came home, I expected there would be big groups of people saying, "Hey, you're back!" but there was nobody. The streets were just normal. The time had passed and the war was over. The war changed Fulton, because a lot of the boys didn't come back. It wasn't the same tempo as before or the same way of life. Of course, we were out of high school, too, so we acted older.

Anyone who was in the war that said they were not scared would be lying. I was fortunate not to have seen combat, thus being very thankful and relieved at the time. I was proud to serve my country, but very fortunate I didn't have to get involved in actual combat. Amen. I felt very bad for those that went before me, particularly a good friend, Bob Pooler, who lost his life. My brother Gerald was also in the Navy before me. He was on the USS Savannah which saw some combat and he would not talk about it. That's the way it was with the ones who saw combat. They wanted to forget the experience.

After that, we all went home and were greeted by Winfred who was not as enthusiastic as Dad had been. I guess the feeling was mutual. I settled in living back there, visiting friends and unwinding. After a short time, my father mentioned that he was shorthanded in the boiler room and asked me to help him out and take the position. I reluctantly agreed to. He was quite relieved to get me off the streets and back into the real world. I contributed to my room and board, but was not required to hand my check over to the household as I was previously.

After work, I went to working out with the barbells and running out back for over an hour to retain my physical gains. Before this time, while in high school, I worked at the Victoria Mill in the boiler room from 4:00pm-10:00pm. In the fall of the year, we would have heavy rains that would get into coal rooms below ground. The Montcalm semi coal truck would deliver several truckloads through the street opening. It was my job to shovel the coal to the back of the large bin to make room for the very large amount of coal coming in for the winter time.

One Saturday morning after carousing Friday night and getting home late, I was very tired. I would work very hard and fast, ahead of the deliveries, then I would take a nap by resting my chin on my hands on the shovel. I realized I was taking a chance, risking that my dad might come around and catch me. As it was, my gamble paid off and he only showed up when I was working the shovel. In fact, that night at supper he bragged to the family how hard I worked. I was lucky that day and dodged the bullet.

After school was another story. Coming in to work after school, I was weak and did not have much energy to the point where I appeared to be lazy. Bob Cole, the foreman, finally complained to my dad who started checking on me. Dad came down the first flight of stairs looking through the window of the steel wall that was part of the storage bin. Of course, there I was dragging my feet, moving slow and shoveling the coal back in the bin. He started bawling me out and told me to "get to work." I reacted in anger and, regretfully, threw a shovel of coal at the wall near the window where he was standing. I knew instantly that I made a HUGE mistake.

Dad immediately turned and came down the last set of stairs and across the 2 x 10 plank used to keep us out of water. He came towards me, and out of desperation I ran towards him and past him without either of us falling off the plank. I went up into the locker room to await my fate. He came roaring in, bawling me out and pounding on me, which hardly phased me. He calmed down some and asked what was the matter with me, being so lazy. I said I was so hungry that it made me weak. I apologized for my actions with the shovel of coal and we talked it over. After that, I was allowed to have a snack before going to work and things turned normal.

Saturdays, I would work eight hours and when I got through, I took a shower to go out with the boys. I remember when I got home and got ready for bed, how the inside of my shirt collar was so black from the coal dust that came out of the pours of my skin. This was in spite of how hard I would scrub with soapy water and showering previously. I can just imagine what was in my lungs, as we did not wear filtering masks.

Chapter 5   College Years

At the end of summer vacation and after graduating from high school, my dad, brother Vincent and I were discussing where I should go to college. I was always interested in Agriculture and hoped to go to Cornell for this. Both my dad and Vince tried to impress on me that the farming industry was not the best money-paying career. They told me I should get into a better kind of work, get established and then get into farming as a hobby. Dad said it would be difficult to get me into Cornell, but he could get me into Syracuse University's School of Forestry. If I really insisted on Cornell, he would try to get me in there. I knew what my dad's choice was for me, so I decided it was best for me to go along with his wishes and chose the Forestry School.

Winifred took me to Syracuse shopping for school clothes. She had a good eye for quality clothes, so we shopped at Wells and Coverly in downtown Syracuse. I ended up with a couple of suits, some other clothes and a camel hair overcoat (THE coat). I lived on University Avenue in a university dorm home. We didn't have a dining room to go to, so we went to a local deli and returned to eat them in our rooms.

We did not come home for weekends. Sometimes, we would go to the girl's dorm and ask for a fictitious name and they would say she did not live there. Well, we told them this girl had said she would help us with English or some other subject and they invited us in. This is one of the ways we got acquainted with girls and made future dates.

Every Saturday morning, we would go on a field trip to learn nature subjects pertaining to Forestry. I would usually end up with a poor grade, but had the opportunity to make it up and barely squeaked by. For some reason or another, my teacher, the Department Head, looked upon me as a playboy type, which I wasn't. I felt his attitude contributed to my poor grades. To prove this, after receiving another poor grade on a field trip I talked to a buddy who got an A into letting me copy his report for my makeup. My grade on the makeup came back as a C. After that, I just did the best I could.

At the end of my high school year, my steady girlfriend, Bea Bernard, who I'd been dating, and I decided to get married before I went back to Canton College. I didn't tell my parents because they would only try to talk us out of it. That night after the wedding, we went to my parents' house to inform them of what we did. As we got into the house, Winifred said to me, "You look like you just

came from a wedding." I answered, "As a matter of fact, we did; it was our own." This took them by surprise, especially my dad, and I felt bad about that. We had some discussion over that and I told them we were staying at Bea's family house until it was time to go to school in the fall.

In the meantime, I was working at the paper mill and I had managed to pick up a 1930 Chevy Sedan from a junk yard ($30). I did an engine overhaul consisting of filing the motor's rod caps. This was a standard procedure done to tighten the bearings after all shims were removed.

Before we did get married, we would go out on dates. One afternoon, we were coming back from Hannibal. We had just picked up a hitchhiker. After we passed through Granby Center, I suddenly did not have any steering, I was helpless. I tried applying the brakes and the car pulled to the left. I had to stop braking to avoid hitting an oncoming car. Fortunately we passed each other with both cars rear ends just touching. Just after that, we veered across the road into the ditch and came to a stop. I looked around for the passenger in the rear seat, and he was gone. We never heard him get out of the car.

Somehow, I got hold of Lee Pooler who was able to lift up the front end of the car with his truck and towed us to Bea's house. Later on, we found the cause of the problem: the nut was missing (besides me) that connected the steering wheel to the steering mechanism allowing the steering to come off. We surmised the junk dealer sold the part, but did not tell me when I purchased the car. We found another nut, attached it to the steering and we were all right. Sometimes, when our car battery would get so low, we would have to push the car to turn over the engine to get it to start.

One night, just outside of Bea's house, we couldn't get it started. We let the car roll back down the hill and let the clutch out, and as I did, there was a snap and we came to a standstill. We got a tow and put the car in her yard until we could get it fixed. The left rear shaft had snapped; not the first time. I searched around for a replacement and we came up with a heavy duty shaft, meant to overcome this problem. Installed it to be free of this problem and it never happened again.

In the fall, when it was time to pack up and drive to school where I had enrolled in Poultry Husbandry, we stopped down to see my dad at the Victoria Mill and say goodbye to him. We discussed how we had gotten married without telling him and how disappointed he was. He gave us $50 as a wedding present and we said our goodbyes and we were off to Canton.

We ended up renting a room on the north end of town. We were allowed to cook our meals on a hot plate and store our food in a small refrigerator. We shared the bathroom with other tenants. Things went along fairly well, but Bea became very lonesome and bored during the day while I was at school. We would come home for the holidays, staying with her folks. While back home, she had our son, which we were all very happy about.

Eventually, I let her talk me into quitting school. She told me we could stay at her folks' place and I could get a job at Nestlé, which I did in the Nestlé Conche Department. This was where the chocolate was milled on machines with two large stainless steel rolls. After it was finished it was loaded in a large portable tub and delivered to large mixers, each having its own special formula. My job was to push these heavy carts to the next station. The chocolate was delivered to the machines where the chocolate was molded into bars and wrapped for shipment.

I was on a three-shift rotation. The 6:00am-2:00pm and 2:00pm-10:00pm shifts were bearable but when it came to the 10:00pm-6:00am shift my system would get upset. It would take me the next two weeks on day and evening shifts to start to feel normal. This was during the hot summer months. It was very difficult for me to get rest during the daytime because we didn't have air conditioning.

Eventually, I was transferred to another department that made the powdered chocolate for hot cocoa and such. One night, they needed somebody downstairs where they were cooking the chocolate. They'd put them in big tins and then on racks on wheels and they'd go right into the oven from there. Cooks would pull them out and my job was to dump them in this grinder. One night, I was working overnight and it was so hot in there. By morning, I was sweating with chocolate dust all over me; just as dark as the chocolate. I decided Nestlé "wasn't my cup of tea" and went back to college.

Eventually, I grew more and more disenchanted with this way of working for a living. I talked things over with my wife and we decided to see if I could get back into school at Canton. I called up Mr. Hicks, head of the Agriculture school, and he didn't see any reason why I couldn't. I had checked into the housing situation and found they had veterans' village, former Army barracks, converted into housing for married students. These living conditions worked out well for my wife because there were other GI families living there.

One day at school, Mr. Hicks called me into his office to talk about my major of Poultry and ask if I would consider changing to Animal Husbandry, this was in dairy. We kicked it around and I decided to change over. One of the subjects was English, which they allowed me to drop without affecting my career.

To supplement my $115 monthly allowance from the Veterans, I took on several part-time jobs: driving school bus on weekends to the games in Potsdam, working in the cafeteria at lunch making sandwiches, midafternoon selling milk from the school's farm out of the cafeteria. I started a refinishing business, working out of the school's vacant milk house they allowed me to use. I also had a couple of fellows working with me there. I worked part time on weekends for an antique dealer. He refinished the furniture using orange shellac. This was a tricky finish to apply as it dried very fast. We didn't have the luxury of drawing it out more than once. Fortunately, I was able to perfect this application, making myself more valuable to the dealer. I had an awful time refusing work on Saturdays because of my school work.

I acquired a job at the local Sheffield Dairy processing plant loading boxcars for shipment. This was the largest processing plant in the world at the time. This area was called the Northern New York milk shed; the glass milk bottle originated in Ogdensburg, New York, not far away.

We were all dirt poor in the veteran's village, but we managed to entertain each other and were content. One time, we bought a pickup truck for the refinishing business. Much to my wife's thinking, it wasn't necessary. She retaliated by buying a new sewing machine on time, which put us up against the wall financially. I eventually had to sell the truck and bought a 1934 Chevrolet Sedan from a fellow student and it turned out to be a good car.

One week, my wife took the baby home for a visit to her folks. The following Friday, I started to drive home during a very heavy wet snow storm. As I drove past Gouverneur there were hardly any cars and my windshield wiper motors couldn't handle the snow. I had to pull over also. I took some light rope and tied it to the driver's side outside wiper and brought it through the window. The car wiper motor was equipped with a vacuum tank. The wipers wouldn't pull up but would retract all because of the wet snow. So I used the rope to pull them up wiping the windshield and the vacuum would pull the windshield wiper back down. This is the means that allowed me to get home with a tired arm. There were many later model cars stranded along the way.

The winters were extremely cold in Canton compared to Fulton, but they did not have the heavy snowfall. One extremely cold morning, a lot of cars couldn't get started. I was a good Samaritan and pulled or pushed them so they could get started. This was all well and good until the following week when my transmission gave out. I acquired a used one to replace it. I could only work 20 minutes at a time installing it. Because of the extreme cold I had to go back inside to warm my hands. It took me most of the day, but I finally got it changed.

My first year back at school, my brother Gerald and wife Betty came to live with us as he had enrolled in an electric course to finish his degree. He had been enrolled in the Milwaukee School of Engineering. Things went along alright, but gradually the situation with two women in the house started getting quite tense. Gerald decided that it was best that his wife should go back to her parents while he finished school.

I recall some medical problems my son had and the local doctor was very good to us. Once, our son developed a problem with his right foot. It started to turn over as he bounced up and down in his teeter babe. The doctor prescribed concentrated cod liver oil and within a week his foot returned to normal. Another time, when my son had a bad cold, we had to take him to be treated by the doctor. We told him we didn't have any money and he said not to worry about it, he said he would make it up along the way.

We had a toy cocker and a tomcat for pets. The tomcat did nothing but go out tomcatting at night and come back and throw up, then eat two or three times as much food as the dog. With my $115 allowance, he was using up quite a share of it. We took him to the vets and had him fixed. He kept on tomcatting for two weeks until one day after he came back home after a night out. He went into our bedroom, came back out and jumped on the back of the sofa, looked at me and really let out a large howl. Getting suspicious, I went into the bedroom and there was a bad smell. We had a large cardboard box with shoes and rubbers stored there. The cat had used this area to relieve himself. We finally gave him away to a farm family.

For my animal husbandry class, we used to take field trips to local dairy farms, inspect them and write up our evaluations. The school owned a dairy farm which we visited for class once a week. We all had to take a turn being the manager for a day. We went on a field trip to a milk machinery manufacturing company Cherry Burrell, in Little Falls. This was the largest plant of its kind. Another time, I drove the school's stake rack truck to the Armory in Troy to pick up furniture and miscellaneous materials allocated to our school. While the truck was being loaded, I noticed a box of fine jack knives. I would have liked to have had one, but would not help myself. After I got back to the school and they were unloading, the foreman took the box of knives and proceeded to give them away, and I actually missed out.

In my last year, during the 4th quarter, I was offered a job at the local Queensboro processing plant, which I substituted for classroom time to fulfill my final year in dairy. I would work in the milk receiving station dumping farmers' cans of milk for processing that day. Part of the job was to examine the cans for faulty product before dumping. On one occasion, when we were moving quite fast, one can looked alright until I dumped it and a lot of scaly milk came out which should have been rejected. All I could do was put a warning tag on the can. After I did, I glanced out the window and there was the guilty farmer grinning at me.

The one good thing about that can of milk was it would be going through sterilization. During the rest of the day, I worked in a lab testing for butter fat content. I had an actual license and was required to sign a tag with my number verifying the quality of the product.

On one occasion, we were producing the first tanker of 50% butterfat content, heavy cream to their plant in New York City. When they got through filling the tanker it was 4 x 40 quart cans short. The foreman topped it off with water. This was actually adulteration and would affect the butterfat content which I was responsible for. Fortunately, the test came out at 49>5% which was right on the border of passing. While working during the testing on other days, I would save the remaining of the test samples and take them home rather than throw them out.

One evening, we decided to make some chocolate ice cream with our hand crank ice cream maker. We cranked the contents which seemed like an extra-long time and finally it solidified. We dished out the ice cream to all of our neighbors, and we all remarked how tasty it was. I got to checking the texture and found that it was actually butter. We all got a big kick out of that. I never figured out why it didn't crank into ice cream other than it was a very hot day.

While at school in Canton, I organized a men's athletic club consisting of eight students. We would do calisthenics, weights, etc. on a regular basis after school.

Canton College Athletic Club. I am on the left and was the Club President.

My Canton graduation with Winifred and Dad.

At the end of my first year I acquired a job at a local veterinarian's home, landscaping his large yard plus removing stones from his cellar floor which he planned to replace with cement. While I was still working at Queensboro dairy coop at Canton, I became acquainted with their field man who took a liking to me and got me a job working at their Canastota milk processing plant. They received their milk from local dairies in tank trucks which I tested for butter fat and percent solids. Some of the milk was processed for heavy cream, butter and skim milk; the latter which was processed into cheese.

I worked in the cheese operation, which was quite interesting. The milk was dumped into large heated stainless tanks which contained a mixing device for mixing ingredients for use in cheese. The first process was cheese curd and the milk was mixed and sterilized right in the tanks. The following day, the cheese maker would add the ingredients, which would cause the milk to coagulate, changing it to solid particles and a watery by product called whey. This was drained off leaving behind a rubbery mass of solids. It was then cut into large slabs, which had to be turned over by hand to drain the remaining liquid. The solids materials were cut up into cheese curd. This was placed in large circular units where they were compressed draining the liquid. These end products were large wheels of cheese that were wrapped in cheesecloth and stored in large freezers for curing over a long given time. My compensation there was $49/week against expenses of $52/wk. I made up the shortfall doing odd jobs.

After a while, my wife became fed up and packed and went home with our son to live with her parents in Fulton. Needless to say, I resigned my job at the coop after receiving a letter of recommendation for wherever I would apply for employment. The situation that prompted my departure was when I found out the company had hired a less qualified young man whose parents were influential with company management. His compensation was $10 above my income. I ended up back home with the family at my wife's parents.

We were able to acquire an apartment at Pooler's farm on West River Road North, just outside of Fulton. We had to share a shower/bath with the family downstairs which worked out OK. Our toy cocker pet was a problem when she came into heat. Male dogs came from everywhere. Finally, one nailed her and she ended up having one male mongrel pup that we gave away. We had her fixed after that.

We also had a pet cat. One wintery evening, we decided to go to the movies. Our kitchen stove was a combination of coal and gas. The coal was a good source of heat. We also had coal heat from the main house furnace. After we came home from the movies, I took the coal scuttle and proceeded to add coal to the fire. Before I realized it, there was water coming out of the coal scuttle and into the fire. Right away I realized it was cat urine. I ended up putting a large amount of it on the fire creating a bad odor that saturated the apartment. We had to use fans, open doors and windows to clear the air.

When it snowed we had to shovel the driveway. Mr. Pooler, our landlord, had a tractor with a blade to help remove the snow. One time I built a wooden snow plow to tow behind my car as an experiment. I had my son sit on it to hold it down to plow more efficiently. The minute I started the plow, the nose caught on a rut and flipped over with my son on it. I stopped right away, and he was luckily not hurt but a little shook up. That ended that experiment.

With my son Tom.

On the farm, we had a problem with rats getting into the cellar. We were forever setting traps and catching them. One night, one worked his way up to our apt and into our bedroom. My wife and son were both standing up on their beds complaining. Mr. Pooler finally came up and killed it by hitting it hard with a shoe rubber. After, we went around plugging any holes that may have given him access to the apartment. One day, I was out shoveling the driveway, and my son said softly, "Dad…" and I looked up and he had a dead rat in his hands and pointing it at me. I immediately told him to drop it and explained to him the dangers of germs, etc. It was a disgusting sight, but I couldn't really get upset with him.

Chapter 6   Working at Sealking

I immediately started applying for a job, particularly at the Sealright Company. Sealright was formed to utilize the Oswego Falls Paper Company's product to make milk bottle caps. The Paper Company was a mill that manufactured many products and was managed by Mr. Frank Ash. At the time, Sealright was manufacturing a vinyl-coated, heat-sealable bottle cap (seal-on) which was used as a protective cover applied to the tops of the glass milk bottles.

Mr. Eugene Skinner, an associate of Mr. Ash's, was influential with the idea of the Sealking vinyl-coated square milk bottle and having it patented. This unique vinyl, heat-sealable carton gave Sealright the edge over its competitors' wax-coated cartons. The Sealking carton was developed through the company's Research and Engineering Department, headed by Mr. Ike Wilcox. Mr. Cliff Morse ran the research lab, assisted by Mr. Bob Ellis.

The Sealking carton was composed of four parts: a double vinyl-coated side wall; a neoprene bottom, which was impregnated and vinyl-coated on the inside; a top, which was vinyl-coated on the inside; and a section of foil with a release coating, which was attached on one corner under the top of the carton. The release coating on the foil allowed the carton's ease of opening. Both the side wall and the top were printed. These cartons were manufactured in Fulton and sold to the dairies, where they were formed and filled on Sealking machines.

The top also had an application of heat-resistant overprint varnish. The side wall part was printed, scored and "blanked" (or cut out) on a purchased rotary cutting machine. These machines were manned by one operator and two packers. The top parts were printed and blanked by one operator and a packer. The bottom parts were double blanked by one operator and two packers. The release-coated foil was purchased in roll form from an outside supplier and then shipped to the dairy, where it was applied to the cartons during the form-and-filling operation.

After a short time had passed, I was called in for an interview. I was hired by Mr. Earl Foster to work in the Sealking quality-control lab, assisting Mr. Chet Belon. I was hired based on my experience at Quality Control as inspector for milk. I ended up working in the newly formed Sealking department in the quality control lab working for their manager.

My duties were to collect previous day's production samples and forming them into a model using their lab forming machine. It would fill them with blue dye solution place them in a humidifier for overnight. In morning, I would evaluate them for bulging and leakage. The final coating used to coat the bottle parts was difficult to apply without ending up with pin holes which were identified with a naphtha dye solution used to test them. Eventually, the research department came up with a polyethylene coating that was extruded on the paper for the bottle parts. It was much superior to the vinyl.

An ink formula had to be made that would adhere and pass all end use tests required. Our main supplier, Converters Ink Company, represented by Oliver Casey came up with an acceptable formula and this allowed us to go into production. The Sealking Department installed an extruder to coat the paper board.

During my first year of employment at Sealking, one of my duties was to stop at the old woolen mill where part of the production was still made. I collected samples from previous day's production. I had a car problem with a throw out bearing going bad in the clutch area. I ended up starting the car in gear as I had no clutch. When I came to a stop light, I turned the key off to come to a stop, then restarted when the light turned green. I did this for two or three days until I could get a new bearing installed. After that, everything was fine. Eventually, I picked up a 1939 Chevrolet sedan from a dependable dealer so I could have good transportation.

As time went on, I was placed in charge of three inspectors per shift who monitored samples from each phase of production. I also was responsible for handling the inks and recommending where to purchase products to the Purchasing Department. I had one person who assisted me with this latter responsibility. We matched colors and mixed up the required quantity for production.

Some of my other duties in Sealking included: writing up procedure for running trials in production, evaluating results and reporting results to key personnel, establishing operating tolerances that were within the capability of the production equipment and its end use (This not only included specific dimensions of the carton's blanks, but also colors and coating), working with the Art Department under Dick VanWalkenberg and John Krystiniak to be sure designs of new artwork were within the realm of the carton, keeping abreast of evolutions in our industry by reading trade journals, and then sharing these articles with our key personnel.

During this time, the research department came up with an impervious polyethylene coating that replaced the vinyl coating, giving Sealright a tremendous advantage. Little did I realize how working in the Sealking would enhance my career in the next phase of my employment. As a matter of fact, this had started to happen a few years earlier. Looking back, this came about both from my experience working as chief inspector and my flexographic ink handling responsibilities.

I was being observed by my future employer, Mr. Oliver Casey, Technical Sales Representative for Converters Ink Company, each time he called on Sealking to run trials on new ink formulations. The Converters Ink Company was an independently-owned company, run by their President, Mr.Karl Beher, and his key personnel, including Mr. Casey. Converters was a fledgling company that had a premium product and highly- qualified technical personnel. It was expanding in a lucrative market and was looking for qualified people to hire. As luck would have it, I seemed to fit the bill.

One might wonder why it took about two years for my transition to the new position to take place. One reason was Sealking's dramatic change in the late '40s from vinyl coating to polyethylene. I was anxious to go through this change to polyethylene because there was a lot of film-printing customers using this product, and so this experience was very valuable to me.

Another reason was my so-called insecurity in changing jobs. Fear of getting out of one's comfort zone can be a natural thing experienced by many, not only in employment, but also in other phases of life. This could include things such as a child learning to walk, the first day of school, leaving home for a job, getting married—the fear of the unknown.

A third reason was Mr. Casey's nervousness in hiring his good customer's key personnel. Sealright was one of his largest accounts and he wondered how management would be: would they resent this and take his business away? Fortunately, Mr. Casey was valuable to Sealright with his technical skills and a quality product. Mr. Casey worked hand in hand with Converters' chemists in developing a flexographic ink, tailored to the needs of Sealking's new and unique product. He actually was a one-man show in the flexographic industry, formulating the ink and adjusting it to work on each customer's product and machinery.

I also want to mention Jim Falanga and Harold Blake, who both assisted me with the Sealking lab duties but at different time frames. Both men were very capable and ambitious.

Chapter 7   Working in Ink Sales

Eventually, these hiring problems were resolved and I made the successful transition to being a technical sales representative for the Converters Ink Company. I gradually overcame my insecurity situation after confiding in two of the Sealking management personnel: Mr. Gene McDaniels, Plant Manager and Mr. Charles Humphrey, General Foreman, who were all for the move. Their final advice to me as a salesman was to be honest and be myself with the customer. This really worked!

I went on to work with Mr. Casey for a period of time, until I branched out on my own for Converters, calling on other customers in the area. My total length of employment as a technical sales representative was 31 years. During that time, Converters Ink had been sold several times and changed its name to ICI Specialty Inks.

In working with potential customers as a newcomer, it was

necessary to sell myself to them, thus building up their confidence in me and, hopefully, interest in purchasing our product. I would always be sure to set up a time with my customers for my next visit and work with them on any conflicts in schedules.

It was important that the customer would look forward to my visits in a productive and entertaining time. In order to accomplish this, I would gather new subjects in the industry from the trade journals I read, along with our company's prints of inks and data. Gradually, as I gained their confidence, they were receptive to my submitting a quantity for trial and evaluation. I always made it a point to be on hand to assist in this run. This procedure led to the sale of our product on a routine basis. As time went on, I became more involved in helping them solve production problems working with their personnel, running training classes on color matching and ink handling.

Along the way, I made contributions to the industry with articles I had written and were published. In August 1964, I was privileged to have an article I wrote on "In-Plant Ink Handling" published in the *National Flexographic and Converting Magazine*. In July 1967, through my customers, I became involved with the Rochester Institute of Technology School of Printing. RIT offered a two-week course in flexographic printing. This course was formed to educate people on flexographic printing and related fields. I was invited to participate in the course as an instructor, using our company's product. During the course, I was privileged to meet many people in the industry and to establish a working relationship with potential customers. Two national magazines, *Flexographic and Converting* and *Modern Converter*, featured an article including pictures on this course. In June 1969, a second of my articles was published in *Flexographic Printing and Converting.*

By 1976, Convertor Ink Company had been sold to Beatrice Foods and became part of their chemical division. Leon Triberti, President of Convertor Ink, nominated me to receive an award for outstanding sales from the President of Beatrice Food Company, Mr. Don L. Grantham. I was flown to Chicago, attended their national sales meeting and received the award.

I had one particular customer in the Rochester area called Specialty Printing. The operator on this one printing press would gauge his press speed by the size of the order. I was coaxing the management to run top speed to be most efficient. I coaxed them into going after a Schuler's potato film print as a customer, which he did. He purchased the inks from my company and told me he expected me to assist in showing the operator how to run the order at maximum speed, which I did successfully.

One evening after a successful production day, I took the manager, Hank Kline, and one of his production personnel out to dinner. This was in summer. After dinner, Hank invited us all to go sailing in his 32' sailboat on Lake Ontario. It was close to sunset.

We sailed into the sunset going westward and as it got dark we turned around and sailed back eastward with a full moon. I was very impressed with how quiet it was except for the sound of the swells made by the boat. It was a very enjoyable evening.

Hank Kline, of the Specialty Printing Company, did work for the Eastman Kodak Company. He introduced the personnel to me and put a good word in for my company's product. I made a call on the Eastman Kodak printing division and met a very fine gentleman, Paul Anasemly, who was in charge and his able assistant Walter Hagen. They were responsible for supplying their company with a four-color mailer envelope. This was used by customers to have their pictures packaged. They gave me a trial order of each of the four colors required and set a trial date for me to come in and assist with it.

I found out I was limited to speed due to the shortcomings of their press. They lacked proper drying of the ink. The first printed color was full coverage of yellow that was not drying fast enough for the succeeding colors to print on top of it. As they tried to get any speed, the colors would offset to the back of the web. I recommended that they re-install the first turn roller further away from the second down color and add dryers.

When I came back in on my next call, they showed me how they had followed my instructions and was now getting proper speed out of the press. This shocked me because most printers were reluctant to make such changes. My lab was surprised with the size of the orders from Eastman Kodak when they started ordering.

On my future calls, usually around lunchtime, we would do business and then go to lunch. We would have a cocktail which they insisted on paying for and I would pay for lunch. At one time, they invited me to play in a golf tournament for the Rochester Printing Club at their local golf course, Brook Lee. I didn't know what to do, being new on the job. I called my lab and told them about the invitation. My boss explained to me that this was part of my sales job. I was relieved and went ahead and had a great time.

Along the way, Paul invited me to meet his wife and adult daughter to have dinner. He had explained ahead of time how severely handicapped his daughter was. She was totally dependent on her parents for everything. I arrived at their home, was welcomed in and introduced to his wife and daughter. I was shocked to see how much of an invalid their daughter was. She couldn't talk but could communicate by making sounds to them. The parents were totally devoted to her. They treated her in a very normal way and this served to put me at ease with the situation. They were wonderful people.

I had another customer that operated out of a multi-story old wooden building in Rochester. He was a tough sell, because his press operator favored his current supplier. I finally coaxed the foreman into a trial and was able to demonstrate to him that my product was superior. He promised to give me business but never seemed to order. I finally asked him why. He said he had such a large inventory of my competitor's ink on hand that had to be used first. It turned out his press operator would go out to dinner as a guest of a competitor who would get him to buy more ink even though they didn't need it. The foreman put a stop to all this and eventually started to order from my company.

I had a customer in Buffalo, Sid Schulman, who owned Transparent Bag and did a lot of film printing and bag making. I would call on him and was invited into his office. I sat in this plush lounge chair and sank down into it so low that I ended up in an intimidating position. After a few visits, I managed to sell him a five-gallon trial pail of red ink. He printed with it and was very impressed. He started purchasing from us.

There was a large film printer in Macedon, New York that was very difficult to sell. They had three divisions: Research and Development, Industrial Bags, and Film Printing. At R&D, our lab developed a priority coating which they used on their polypropylene film developed for snack wrappers (crackers, Hostess Twinkies, etc.). The industrial division extruded polypropylene into vegetable and fertilizer bags, covers for dry cleaner clothes. They did this with two -four color Flexo print stations in line.

These print stations were necessary, but received the least

attention. Consequently, this presented the most problems. This is where my printing experience came in handy. Lou Johnson, superintendent, asked me to go out on the line and help straighten out their problems.

A Flexo print station included a pan to hold the ink, a rubber fountain roller immersed in the ink and used to carry the ink up to the steel anilox roll composed of cells to transfer the correct amount of ink to the printing plate roll that transferred it to the web against a steel backing roll. The rubber fountain roll was geared to run slower than the anilox roll to act as a metering action. The ink station had a cover over the rollers to reduce premature solvent evaporation from the ink. Each color station had a circulating ink pump immersed in the five-gallon supply pail.

As the ink circulated through the station and back to the pump it would always have a tendency to get thicker by loss of solvent through evaporation. The pressman controlled this by checking the viscosity with a test unit called a Zahn Cup which contained a drain hole that they used to time how long it took for the ink to drain. He used a stopwatch to do the timing which was usually 18 to 20 seconds. He would do this usually every 20 minutes. As the ink got heavier, solvent was added to bring the viscosity back under control. In order to check the colors for proper shade, the pressman would take small web samples containing all printed colors attach them to a cardboard side by side, identify time of sampling, and thus would have a visual control for all the day's production to be filed for reference in case of any customer complaints. In checking the line out for any printing problems, I found instances where the fountain cover was riding against the anilox roller, wearing it down by friction.

Some of the operators would ignore viscosity, letting the inks get thicker and causing a dirty print, poor drying and ink offsetting on the back of the product. I set up a procedure for making sure the print rollers were in parallel, resulting in an even impression which led to a sharp print. This is called a 'kiss impression', like a mother-in-law kiss. Eventually, I ended up writing procedures for the pressmen to follow and maintain quality print.

Before I was established in selling to them, I had some help from one of our salesmen calling on them with me. He had lost his license for a short period of time, so the company assigned me to work with him, driving to his accounts in New York City and New England, as well as to my accounts. This was a break for me because it gave me on-the-job training in sales, as well as to build up my confidence.

I remember calling on one of his shoebox accounts where they were working on color matching a certain shade of tan. Each time I made an adjustment to the ink, the operator would run off a few print samples and check the adjusted color print to the standard, using the north light as an ideal representation. It was late in the afternoon and the outside light began to fade, forcing us to use inside light for the color match. As a result, the fluorescent light caused the shade to change. As it was, we went to their lighting, the closest match to northern daylight and we achieved a comparable match. We learned a valuable lesson.

At Kordite, in Macedon, which turned out to be Mobil Chemical through acquisitions, we made a call on Mr. Mel Cagen, operations manager. Mr. Cagen, fortunately for us, had a friendly relationship with Sid Schulman from Transparent Bag in Buffalo. Sid had previously contacted Mel about print quality results he had using our inks that I had sold him. Actually, Mel wanted to give us a trial order and told us he would do so. As a shocker to Mel and myself, Walt said yes. We had these promises before from Mel's technical person responsible for whom to order from. He had developed such a friendly relationship with a competitor that he would not follow through to order from us. This was protecting his friend's business.

When Mel heard Walt's comments, he became disturbed and told Walt that when he told us we would get a trial order, he meant it. I wasn't sure of how things would happen with Walt's reverse psychology, but Mel did follow through and we were granted the trial. We shipped the trial of red ink to be used on mesh print for vegetables. I assisted in the trial and I asked the pressman to leave all the press settings for our ink product as with their current supplier for a good comparison in print quality with our competitor.

The pressman printed the first few bags with our ink, resulting in missed printing, just as if he had backed off on the print impression. I assumed he did this and asked him why. He remarked he had not adjusted any settings and this resulted in being in our favor. It showed that our ink could run in a thinner thickness resulting in a cleaner print and better ink mileage. We had the operator adjust the ink impressions demonstrating this. This sold them on our product and we became their supplier.

Fortunately, Mel did not resent Walt's comments and followed through on his word. All of this occurred in the Industrial Division. As it was, they developed a film division and bought several 6 color central impression presses to accomplish this. They first printed bread bags in large volumes and they added other products such as snacks, meat wraps, Hostess Twinkies, etc. The meat wrap was printed on the reverse side of the film and backed up with two layers of white ink in order to block the visual effects of the meat.

I happened to be in the area working on some problems. As it was, their technical man happened to be on hand with that run. He came over to me and showed me the product with two layers of white used to mask the visual effects of the meat product. He jokingly asked me if our white ink could produce the same effect with only one layer of our white ink. I thought for a minute and knew that by increasing the viscosity of our white ink it would give them opacity needed and net good quality printing. He told me he was just pulling my leg, assuming that we couldn't do it. So I had challenged him to give us a trial to prove it, and he did. We made the trial early in the evening on a snowy Friday night. As it turned out, it was successful with one white application. He was in disbelief of the results, but agreed our product was acceptable. He couldn't bring himself to give us a production order until early the following week. I remember driving home late that night after dark, elated with the outcome, the large snowflakes hitting my windshield sort of mesmerizing me.

Convertors Inc. was founded by Mr. Karl Behr, from Princeton, New Jersey. He also maintained a family residence in New York City. Mr. Behr formed the company with three other knowledgeable people: Mr. Curt Cole, head chemist; Mr. Jerry Klein, who ran the lab and Mr. Oliver Casey, technical sales. These people worked for a larger ink company called IPI.

Mr. Behr's grandfather was connected with the Behr Manning Abrasive Company in Troy, New York. Karl inherited his grandfather's fortune and thus had funds to form the Convertors Company, as well as hire the three other people. He founded it on the basis of customers that he and Mr. Casey knew were loyal to them and switched their business to convertors. One of the large companies was Sealright, out of Fulton, that had branches across the country. Mr. Behr eventually expanded and built plants in key areas across the country to give better service to their key customers.

Mr. Casey was a one man show in regards to the fact he would understand his customers' problems, take them to the Linden factory in New Jersey, help the lab formulate the ink, manufacture it and bring back the products in five-gallon pails to the customer. He would then supervise testing and the production run at Sealright.

Mr. Casey was the gentleman responsible for recruiting me to work for the Convertors Ink Company, originally as his assistant, and later on my own covering most of the Upstate New York customers. I remember how difficult it was for me to get sales. I finally got a five-gallon trial order from Transparent Bag in Buffalo. And when I went to Linden for our sales meeting, I walked into the lab and got a rousing cheer from the people for my successful first order. This was arranged by Mr. Cole, head chemist, to give me a boost in self-confidence. It was all uphill after that, especially with Mr. Behr calling on customers with me and with Walt at other times. Sales started to come. Curt was an outstanding chemist and was responsible for the superior product we were able to sell the customers.

There was a National Flexographic Technical Association we belonged to. An annual meeting was held each year in key cities, New York, Chicago, Kansas City, Boston, Atlanta, and also in Montreal and Toronto. I attended all of these with my key customers (Kordite/ Mobil Chemical). We would go to various seminars pertaining to subjects about the industry. I would entertain the customers afterwards, taking them to a nice restaurant and sometimes to a good show. If I didn't do this, they were fair game to competition.

On one occasion, our new president, Leon Triberti, decided that our salesmen didn't need to attend and he would go instead of us. On my sales call to Macedon, talking to the operations manager, I asked him how things went at the convention. He proceeded to tell me about his experience with our president who was entertaining them. A customer discussing the industry in general asked the president what Converters Ink was going to do for them this coming year. Our president seemed to be annoyed by the question and replied as to what Mobil Chemical was going to do for Converters Ink. This was not the diplomatic thing to do.

The Operations Manager explained his reaction to this personally: If our president wanted to act this way, the customer said he would enjoy the meals that our president was offering, but he didn't have to buy our product. When he got back to Macedon and had his first meeting with key personnel (this included his boss and others), he proceeded to tell them all about his experience with our president and told them what he had told me. So, here I was with my main customer and about to lose them all because my main boss's comments. I couldn't go to him and chew him out for his remarks, so I just continued my job servicing the customer and, as fate would have it, the customer apparently overlooked the ill treatment and continued to buy our product as if this didn't happen.

Eventually, our company, which was a chemical division of Beatrice Food, was purchased by Imperial Chemical of Great Britain which owned Glidden Paints as one of its products. They established ICI of America with us being in Chemical Division. While we were still owned by Beatrice Foods, our Converters Ink president, Leon Triberti, recommended me to go to the Chicago Beatrice Annual Meeting and be inducted to the President's Club for outstanding sales of the year, one of three in the US. When I got up to receive my award, President Grantham presented it to me in front of all the other company reps and asked me how I achieved these outstanding sales. I told him I was scared to death (meaning being scared of failure) and followed up telling him it was being a good listener and following up on promises and servicing them.

Receiving my award from Mr. Grantham.

Just after we were purchased and became Convertor's Ink Specialty Company of ICI America. The new company had a national sales meeting attended by the new company's president. We went into the room with tables and chairs set up in a rectangular shape or with one side containing the speaker's podium. We all filed in and took our seats. The Convertors president had a seat several chairs to my right. Not realizing why our new ICI president chose to sit by me in the chair to my right and I introduced myself. Samples of prints containing our inks were passed around and as our new president received them, he would ask me many technical questions about them. Thank the Lord I was able to answer them correctly.

I happened to notice, Mr. Triberti looking in our direction and glaring at me. I guess he resented our new president asking me about all the technical areas of our inks. I was a victim of circumstances. I just couldn't refuse our main boss's questions and tell him to ask Leon. On the flight back to New Jersey, Mr. Triberti would not speak to me and acted as though I didn't exist.

As time would have it, he seemed to get over it. Apparently the ill feeling between him and new president of ICI continued to exist. Eventually, ICI America became Zeneca Specialty Inks and Mr. Triberti remained as president. One day, he resigned and went to work for a main competitor, Sun Chemical. We were all most certain he took much proprietary information, pricing and formulas with him. Earlier, before this came about, we lost our brilliant chemist, Curt Cole to cancer and Convertor's hired a Mr. Tony Cappucio as head chemist, who was a very capable gentleman. When Mr. Triberti left, Tony felt he should become president and let it be known that if he didn't become president, he would go to work for our competitor, Sun Chemical.

Well, as it worked out, ICI America's president selected our Canadian president, Bill Bulmer to fill the spot. Sure enough, Mr. Cappucio resigned and went to work for the competitor. Mr. Bulmer was hired from Mobil Chemical, where he worked for R& D before that he worked himself up from where he worked as a very good pressman. It was quite a success story, working his way up without a college education. While he was at Mobil he was in charge of running ink trials of three different suppliers, evaluating one against the other. As it was, Convertors came out on top and we maintained our business. Earlier on, when Mr. Triberti was still president, I had an account Climax Mfg. in Lowville. We were their main supplier and they were to run comparative trials and entertain contracts from Sun Chemical, who had a very capable man that submitted a proposal. My company chose not to do the same, which left me in a very vulnerable position. I went to work and drew up my own proposal with the help of one of our technical field men, Mr. Les Zahner. Les pulled all the info from our company and put it together in a proposal format. He and I set up a meeting with Climax representatives and made the proposal and won the contract. One of the stipulations was that I would work at their plants servicing once a week, which I was doing anyway. This was a tough experience but a good education.

There was another large company, American Can, out of Neenah, Wisconsin, that moved to Scranton. Our sales director had called on them in WI when he worked for our competitor< IPI. He was instrumental for getting Convertors in on the business. We made our presentation to them. As a stipulation, I would call on them once a week for service. They were a direct competitor to Macedon and had six color CI (Central Impression) presses. Frank assured them that there would not be any problem of confidentiality with me calling on both competitors. He described me to them as having the host of diplomacy.

Another one of my main customers, Little Falls Color Print, in Little Falls, New York, printed both flexographic and Rotogravure. They decided to run competitive trials between our company and a competitor, who their VP was bent on winning. If he did, he would go to work for them. The competitors ran their trial with two technical people. When it came time for our test, it happened to fall on my vacation time, which was overdue. Our lab assigned one of our men to fill in for me. As it was, the trial date fell on some holiday time, however, Little Falls insisted on running the trials as scheduled. All of the trial inks were on hand. Our man Tony ended up calling Mr. Triberti and asking if he could be excused, and he approved. This left me without a means to compete.

When I got back from vacation and called on Little Falls, they told me what had happened. I was furious but my hands were tied. As it was, the Little Falls management granted me another chance to run our trials. This was an around the clock, intense job. There were four four-color jobs that I had to mix up colors for and they lasted about four hours each. I had a motel where I could rest while each job was running. I made it through and maintained my business with them. The VP went to work for a competitor's business and was not a threat to my business in the area.

The Sealright Company was another story. Mr. Casey continued to service it and not let me help. When he retired, it was like starting over with a new account. Our local company, Morrill Press, a rotogravure printer, expanded and built a large plant. They also hired a competitor who worked for a competitive ink company with business there. I kept calling on them and we were able to take over some of the business with Mr. Joe Greenberg, a roto ink chemist. He would come up on a monthly basis and run trials. Usually, I would call on them on a weekly basis from the sales end.

After my retirement, our company eventually had a good business relationship with Morrill Press. This company was eventually sold to a company called Spears, which printed beer labels. It was all a proprietary process. Prior to this, our company hired a young man as technical person to work for Convertor's at Morrill's due to the load on Mr. Greenberg The gentleman was very technically savvy and was able to break into Morrill's personal computer records. Mr. Bob Bymaster, Morrill's plant manager, ordered him immediately out of the plant. Our company replaced him with one of their capable lab technicians.

I had a large flexo-roto printer of dog food bags an old account of Mr. Casey's who had neglected it for the Sealright account. Plant superintendent Fred Perkins remembered Mr. Casey and was favorable to me and tried to get our company in on the business. One of their big accounts was Ralston Purina, which they were running roto with water inks. I was granted a trial on it.

I assisted getting the trial running using our water ink formulation and extending varnish (ink without color). I was not sure how far I should go with straight water or water and extender varnish. I called my lab and told them I got good color match at a certain viscosity using just water. They told me this should be OK. The customer went ahead, running several large production rolls of product. When it came time to convert them into large bags, they discovered bad ink offset on the inside of the product which was entirely unacceptable. My immediate question to the customer was "Didn't your quality control test show this?" They remarked that they did not run such tests. Our company had insurance that would have covered this loss, but they refused to apply it to this situation to help our customer. We lost that business. As it turned out, the problem was with the colors too low in percent solids and should have been run with a higher viscosity using extending varnish to maintain solids to dry the ink.

Before this, in another situation, they were running another order using solvent-based ink successfully, but were due to run out of ink before truckers could deliver to them on time. Their press foreman, Mr. Walter Wicks, who I had become friends with, offered to drive me to our factory in Linden with his truck, which we did. We got the product to the customer on time and saved the day. The only problem was Walt's company refused to compensate him for his expenses. We took care of it.

We had a large account, Georgia Pacific, in Plattsburg that used a Flexo printer on tissue for toweling, toilet paper, and napkins. I started them printing with inks and they ended up ordering one truck load each month. One of the Georgia Pacific's technicians started playing around with our formulation to overcome one of their end use problems. He corrected the problem and recommended that we incorporate the ingredient into our formula, which we did. This was a HUGE mistake.

After Georgia Pacific printed with this new formula, it was adjusted and sent out to the customer. The printed product developed a putrid odor when opened. I went to Plattsburg to check out the problem and called my lab from there. The problem didn't seem to sink in.

I drove to Albany with an unopened box of product and flew to New Jersey to demonstrate the problem to the lab. As soon as they opened the product, they got a snout full of the putrid odor. As a result, we lost their business, but fortunately they went to our sister company, Blacker Ink Co., out of Montreal. I was told by my company that I could still call on the customer, but couldn't compete against Blacker. As time went on, after a couple of years calling on the purchasing agent, he told me Blacker had some problems and failed to address them with Georgia Pacific. I told my company this and they OK'd me to go after the account, which I did and was able to get the business back with a revised formulation.

I called on another tissue printer, Vanity Fair, in Groveton, New Hampshire, which was one of Walt's that he turned over to me. Plant manager of Georgia Pacific Plattsburg told me about a tissue manufacturer outside of Gouverneur, New York. I called on the manager, Clint Fisk, and set up an initial trial order for their start up. We did all this and set up a procedure to set the ink pan roller and the analox roller in parallel and how to adjust the inks. I also showed them how to take small web samples on every roll produced and mount them on cardboard for a roll-to-roll color comparison.

One day, I got a call from Mr. Fisk telling me my inks were giving them printing problems. I called on him right away. When I got there, I waited in his office for him to finish up some business. I said hello to him and told him how bright and cheery his office was from a recent coat of paint. He said, "Never mind the GD problem. Get down to the press and straighten out the ink problem."

When I got down to the press and looked at the print, it was all squashed out. I immediately asked the foreman if he used the brass thickness gauge to set the roller compression. He said that he had. I had him back off an impression at all critical points until the print started to come in without all the ink pressure. Come to find out, the foreman investigated the print plate order and found the plate company screwed up and made them to a higher thickness and out of specifications. By this time the plates were pretty well squashed out but we managed to get a halfway acceptable print until he was able to get a new set up printing plates with the proper specification.

Another time, we had trouble getting 20 barrels of ink to him past Utica, New York. I rented a stake rack truck, went to Utica, picked the barrels up, loaded them by hand and delivered them to Mr. Fisk on time. While I was unloading these by hand, I overheard Mr. Fisk talking to one of his employees, joking about how I was out there doing the unloading by hand. At least I proved to him I could get the product to him on time, no matter what. After that, we had a more mutual relationship.

I used to call on Mobil Chemical during the week, whenever I was needed, but always on a Friday to take Lou Johnson and staff to lunch at the Hotel Sellen in Palmyra. I would take Lou and his wife, Pat, to dinner that evening and ended up staying overnight at their house, driving home on Saturday morning. They had four daughters and a son, and I experienced their growing up.

One time, when staying overnight at the Johnson's house, Pat mentioned that her clothesline was awkward to use. So I decided to install a more efficient set up without asking. I wanted to surprise them. I had two poles made up with a 'T' shape and hooks. I loaded them on top of my company car and drove over one morning. I dug the holes and put the poles up in place. They were both pleased and surprised to have a new efficient clothesline.

One evening, we went out to dinner during the week, not a Friday, and ended up at their house before my drive home. Their neighbor had a very nice buckskin horse and all the kids were taking rides. Lou invited me to ride also. I had a pair of dungarees which I had for work and changed into them. I had previous experience riding, but not much. As soon as I swung into the saddle, the horse squatted and took off at a dead run down the gravel road in front of their house. I did not dare rein him in in fear of his suddenly stopping and my flying over the top of him, face first on a gravel road. I gave him the reins and after a short time pulled him to a full stop. He turned and we headed back to Lou's house, where he came to a stop and I got off. Lou felt very bad about how the horse acted and was glad I didn't get hurt. Apparently, the horse had been broken in by someone my weight who had control of him.

As I drove home that evening, I noticed the seat of my pants was wet. After I got home, I dropped my pants to examine and show my wife. They were soaked through with blood. I cleaned up and doctored my rear end and it healed up fine. When telling anyone about the experience, I told them I rode on my right cheek going and my left cheek going back.

The Mobil group had a golf and bowling league that I played in. Everyone had a great time. One Saturday, I worked at the plant on a problem they were having. I got a call from Lou, who told me he and his crew were out on Canandaigua Lake fishing as a guest of my competitor. Lou was doing this as a joke. I responded by saying that I would rather earn his business doing service for him getting more production out. It was all done in good spirits and my business went on.

On one occasion, I took Lou, Harry Mosher, his technical man, to our Linden plant to show them how the ink was made and meet our personnel. At the time, I was driving a Ford Sedan, as a company car that Carl Beher purchased. Everything went alright on the visit. On our return trip, we stopped at a thruway station for a break. Harry and I went in and Lou stayed in the backseat of the car.

When we got back to the car, Lou was sitting up in a blanket of fog and blinking his eyes. The motor burned oil and sometimes this happened. As we got moving the air cleared and, fortunately, Lou was not offended. After we got back, Harry was not too complementary to the Mobil people on our facility. He thought we were not modernized enough. Lou said he didn't care if we made ink in a dishpan, as long as it met their specifications.

Along the way, I naturally got acquainted with all his personnel. One gentleman, Bob Kornbau, stood out in his job and was promoted to Lead Foreman. I got to know him very well and worked closely with him. Bob and his wife, Edna, had three very nice children: Rick, Kathy and Garry.

Mobil had a foams plant in Canandaigua making foam trays for food industry and Lou was promoted to manage it. Bob Kornbau was promoted to Lou's position in Macedon. Mobil purchased several six-color CI printing presses which was under Bob's supervision. Therefore, I spent a lot of time with him working at the plant and entertaining him and his wife. We used to go to a very nice Italian restaurant, Caruso's, in Canandaigua. There were a lot of times Bob would decline and tell me to go on home to my family.

Bea, and I went to Bob Kornbau's for a weeklong vacation. We flew into San Francisco for a little sightseeing. Lo and behold, when Leon Tiburtyi heard about our trip he arranged for our LA manager, Pete Beardsley, and his wife to meet up with us and do the town. Pete took us to The Street of Roses, which was a long block on a steep hill with a winding road; all flowers. It was very beautiful. We ended up having dinner at the Mark Twain Hotel Restaurant at the top, called the "Top of the Mark." It was the highest point in Frisco, what a view. My wife and I were both thrilled. The next day we flew to Bakersfield to visit Bob and his family. At the time his youngest son, Garry, was living with them at home. Bob took us all over the area, which was very nice. I almost drove Edna crazy because I was so wound up.

On another occasion, Bob, Edna and my wife, Bea, went to Toronto to attend a Flexographic annual seminar. We stayed at the Valhalla Motor Lodge. They had an above ground swimming pool and had a downstairs bar built around the glass bottomed swimming pool. So you could sit at the bar and observe the swimmers. One afternoon, Bob and I were sitting at the bar and noticed a newlywed couple swimming around. The husband kept trying to lift his wife by his toe to her behind. She kept pushing him away and they eventually stopped. The bar was fairly crowded and everyone got an eyeful. I could just imagine how the couple would've felt if they knew they were putting on an innocent show for all at the bar.

On one occasion, Mobil had ordered a new six-color CI press in Green Bay, Wisconsin. Bob's head engineer, Dan Olenych, went out to Green Bay to approve it and I was invited with my inks to be used in his presses. Everything worked out fine. We would all go out to dinner in the evening. One time, we had a tour of the city and going by their football stadium, we observed Bart Star working out, running around the stadium to keep in shape.

On another occasion, one of the Maguire sisters, Patty, was doing a single performance at the Three Rivers Inn in Phoenix. I invited eight of the key Mobil personnel and their wives to attend, which they did. We had a table just off the stage. After one song, Patty invited one lucky guy to come up on stage so she could sing to him. As luck would have it, our waitress grabbed onto me and took me up onto the stage. As I went up the stairs, I intentionally stumbled and went on up. Patty introduced herself and asked my name, and I said, "Charlie." I looked down at my table of guests and gave them a down low hand wave. She sang to me on my left side and then said she would change to my right side, which she did. When done, she allowed me to kiss her on the cheek and thanked me for being quiet. We all had a great time and I got a big thrill.

The week after I had received my Beatrice Foods' Presidential Award, I made my call on Mobil. At the time, a Mr. Carl Palone was in charge of the ink department. He was a very technical savvy person. A Mr. Gordon Mosher (Harry's Brother) was General Foreman of the print department. The three of us decided to go to lunch and celebrate my award, as they were responsible for a large part of my sales. We went to a nice restaurant in Canandaigua that we had frequented on other occasions. We all indulged in one of our favorite beverages, a Black Russian, and slightly overdid it, but we had a great time and got back to the plant safely.

On another occasion, I called on Mobil films on a special production run that lasted until 10:00pm. I was working on one of the presses run by Mr. Thomas Tolleson, a very capable operator and an easygoing person. After I arrived home, I realized I had left my briefcase back at Mobil. I called there and talked to Mr. Tolleson and asked if he would take care of it. He not only said he would, but promised to drive it to my house, 60 miles away, after his night shift was complete. When he arrived at my house with it, I took him out and we had a nice breakfast. I was very grateful.

After I had retired, Tom eventually came to work for my company in my old job. I was hired back as a consultant to handle the same job and eventually work with the new salesman. Before Tom came on the company hired another capable gentleman who was an avid golfer. When calling on the Climax account, they opened up the business for bids between us and Sun Chemical. Sun had offered them a color computer system as part of their proposal. A Mr. John Kristofiak was our plant manager at the time and would not counter the offer. Our company had me call on them and try to win the contract. It was actually too late and it went to the competition. Our salesman left the company and Tom was hired.

On one occasion, Tom and I were calling on an account in the Glens Falls area. We were calling on a Mr. Jeff Washburn who was manager for a Valcour account that made placemats. While meeting in his office, I had a mild TIA. I felt the tingling in my arm, but endured it until the end of our meeting. I told Tom and he took me right away to the emergency room at the Glens Falls Hospital. I had very high blood pressure, which they treated me for and got it under control. After that I was all right, but when I got home, I reported to my doctor who set me up on a controlled treatment that has been working ever since. I suffered one set back, when I applied for Long Term Health Care Plan. They charged me $400 more per year on the premium because of the TIA.

One person I used to team up with on the job was Jim Morton of Matrix Company that made Flexo Printing Plates. Jim had Georgia Pacific in Plattsburgh as a very good customer. Same as I did, only with inks. We would get together when we come in contact. We discussed different accounts which were mutually helpful. We became very good friends through retirement. Jim and his wife moved to Florida and we eventually drifted apart.

Another gentleman, Steve Stewart, who owned Baker Adhesive Company, was selling adhesive to Climax Manufacturing in Lowville that made boxes for Macy's, etc. I was selling our inks to them. Steve and I became very good friends. I was to meet him one day at the customer's in Lowville. When he arrived, we visited and he told me had been swimming at the YMCA in Binghamton on the way up. He put a bug in my ear about swimming being a good way to keep in shape. That was in 1988 and I have been doing this three times a week since.

When I went to our plant in Jersey for a sales meeting, Steve and I would meet up and have dinner later. He finally retired and has since passed away. I am still maintaining friendship with his son, Doug. Doug has his own company making coatings and is doing very well. Almost all of our contacts have been over the phone or by letter. We plan to meet up, have dinner and chat about things in general. He has recently made a generous donation to our Green Team to support our cause. (See more about our Green Team later in the book.) This was strictly volunteer on his part, unsolicited.

Chapter 8　　The House on Batavia Ave

As time went on, we decided to have a house built so we could get away from renting. We purchased a lot on Batavia Avenue through a contractor who was going to build the house for us. It was a basic ranch: three bedrooms, a bath, kitchen, dining room and front room, no garage. We chose shake siding to save a couple hundred dollars over clapboards. The shakes were stained and eventually became a problem painting them. Over time, I had them removed and replaced with clapboard, which was a huge improvement for maintenance.

We ran into a problem with snow sifting through the louvers in the attic. This became apparent when water came through the ceiling on the west end of the house when a series of warm days melted the snow and water soaked through the ceilings. I opened up the attic trap door and found the problem. I put a large tub on the floor directly under that entrance (opening). I went up into the attic with a shovel and removed the accumulated snow one shovel at a time. I rolled up the soaked insulation and carried it through the trap door and dropped it into the pan below.

There was a problem with the insulation ringing itself out as I carried it. This compounded the leaking problem. I eventually removed the rolls of insulation and used heaters and fans to dry the area out. I had to put new rolls of insulation down and cover the area of the louvers with plastic to keep the snow from coming in. I eventually installed a small louver that was designed to let the air in and not the snow. We dried the ceilings and walls out downstairs and painted the ceilings affected by the moisture. I had to frequently shovel the roof due to the heavy snow accumulation. It was necessary to re-shovel the snow piles created from accumulated roof snow. We also had a problem of ice forming on the edges of the roof. I installed heat tapes and added a lot more insulation in the attic. This helped but was not a cure all.

We eventually decided to add a two-car garage on the west end of the house. I hired Mr. Rounds a retired carpenter. He only charged us $400 for labor for the whole job. I was his helper. He did a lot of figuring in his head by talking out loud. I would ask him what he said and he would tell me to be quiet because he was figuring. I eventually took the hint and kept quiet.

When it came time to put the roofing on, we were able to put on base of rolled roofing with the weather in our favor. We planned on installing shingles on a Saturday, but unfortunately had a heavy rainfall. This did not stop Mr. Rounds and we installed it in the rain, anyway. Mr. Rounds assured me that this would not be a problem because it would dry out eventually and he was right.

I dug the trenches three or four feet deep for a garage foundation. We hired a cement truck to deposit the base. I had some helpers with wheel barrows to distribute the cement to foundation. I previously installed 2 x 4s forms at the bottom of the ditch to keep the foundation level and correct. My neighbor helped me lay out the proper dimensions with the cement blocks. I laid the blocks over time and installed the base plate on top of them.

After the garage was built, I prepped the dirt floor, leveling it, etc. We had stones brought in for a proper base. I installed an outside cellar door entrance. I built an extra wide stairway to the cellar. I capped the block wall installing receptacle for a movable iron fence. This worked out very well, especially when we had to remove the fence to put large objects down cellar. I had double garage doors installed front and back, along with two regular entrance doors front and back side. I decided to pour a cement floor two out of four sections at a time.

My dad told me he didn't think I could do it. He was actually giving me a challenge. The first two sections went alright. When it came to pour the second two sections, we ended up with heavy winds blowing debris that fell on the wet floor, making it difficult to finish off the floor properly. With the help of my dad, we hung the front and back doors, a product he was selling. They were called Fulluma and consisted of aluminum frames and fiberglass construction. They were very light to handle, but durable in storms. I had a black top driveway installed that was nice for removing snow.

With the garage installed, it created a problem with the snow blowing over the back of the garage and dumping it right in front of it. It was a job removing the snow by hand. Gradually the banks on the side of the driveway built up so high that I couldn't shovel over them. I ended up having to climb up onto the banks and shoveling them back to make room for the snow removal from driveway.

We had problems with ice forming on the eaves on the back of the house, requiring removal. I did it with a hatchet and caused damage to the roof. I eventually installed aluminum strips along the edges and more insulation in the attic to cut down on heat escaping to the attic and melting the snow on the roof. All of this helped but was not a cure-all. I ended up installing heat tapes which helped melt the snow and ice buildup on the edge of the roof. As time when on, I finally purchased a snow blower, which relieved me of a lot of shoveling.

Earlier on, living at the Batavia Avenue house, water came in around the perimeter around the cellar walls and actually up through cracks in the basement floor. I had a city drain in the floor but the problem was getting the water to the drain. I did some research and I learned about placing drain tiles on the inside edge of the floor all around the perimeter of the cellar floor. I rented a cement saw and proceeded cutting the cement 12 inches in from the cellar wall around the perimeter so I could make a trench to lay drain pipe and channel the water to the inside drain. I also punched holes through the bottom of the inside wall to the outside to make a path to relieve the water pressure on the outside.

In reality, we were making what is called a floating slab out of the floor, which was not uncommon practice. After I got the cement cut, I rented an air compressor and an air hammer, and proceeded to break up the cement floor in the trench area. The problem then was getting the residue up out of the trench and discarded. I got some five-gallon pails to do this. My neighbor, Blanchard Shaver, was retired and came over and proceeded to empty debris in them. I hired three of our neighbor's young boys to carry the pails up out of the cellar into a trailer to be hauled away.

As we were working along, I suggested taking a break, so they all started for the stairs. I told them to stop and each carry a pail full of debris so as not waste to a trip emptyhanded. They all grumbled, but did as I asked.

We finally got the trench cleaned out to the proper depths for installing the drain. I waited until the trench was ready and then proceeded to open up the base of the wall outside the cellar stairs. This relieved the water pressure outside the base, where it was being held back. The water just rushed through to the inside, draining it and emptying out. I proceeded bringing in crushed stone as a base and laid the pipe so that it was just below the underside of the cellar floor. I laid tar paper over the pipe and added some more crushed stone and filled cement in over the pipe, completely filling the trench. While I had the trench open, I noticed a laundry tub drain pipe that was broken from before, so I proceeded to repair it before we closed up the cement floor. Thus the project was a success and eliminated the water leak to the cellar floor.

Chapter 9   Green's Candies

Dad's second, middle brother, Harry lived local. In the winter months, he and his wife, Aunt Bessie, would make the Green's hard and cream candies. The cream candies were very intense in labor. He sold candy to local stores and at the old-time Recreation Park Summer Fair. He delivered the hard candy packed in round airtight metal containers. In summer months, Harry did similar work as Uncle Fred.

As I got older, I used to help Uncle Harry with the candy making. He was located on Hannibal Street across from the North End Paper Company. Uncle Harry had a 2-story barn in back of the house with the candy making on the second floor. In the summer months he would make homemade ice cream and sell it and the candy. Aunt Bessie was a teacher in Sterling and had summers off. She would help with the ice cream making and selling it and candy to the local folks. Eventually, Uncle Harry developed heart problems and stopped the candy making and moved out in the country outside of Sterling.

I remember we would occasionally be invited to supper there. After supper, we would sit in parlor and Uncle Fred would smoke a cigar. His belief was to smoke it in the house and his wife was expected to put up with it. Eventually his health became worse and they moved to Zephyr Hills Florida and he later died there.

I decided to carry on the candy business. Uncle Harry willed everything to me with the understanding that I would give Aunt Bessie one cent on every pound sold. Later on, she released me from this obligation. In 1965, Dad went to visit Aunt Bessie and to ask her about the candy operation, etc. This helped me tremendously. I finished off a room in the cellar and set up the operation with the help of our neighbor's son, Mike Durfey, one of four boys: James, William, Michael and Lance.

I would work setting up, get tired and sort of discouraged after working at the Sealking division of Sealright. Mike used to encourage me by saying "Come on Mr. Green, you can do it." Mike later grew up and became a male nurse with outstanding skills in the burn unit of a hospital in San Diego where he and his wife moved to. I started experimenting with the different formulas and it happened to be during the Blizzard of '66 when we were snowed in for a week and didn't have to go into work at Sealright. One of those days after I had been doing the humbugs (candy with molasses and peppermint flavor), Mike's mother Millie called from across the street asking if I had been making humbugs, because their dog Poochie was saturated with the strong humbug odor, which, by the way, was a very pleasing smell. Poochie had been over that day laying outside our north cellar window and was basking in the exhaust smell.

The Cracker Barrel Fair was formed by Vita Chalone of the Lee Memorial Hospital Auxiliary to raise money for hospital equipment. The Fair was held at the War Memorial Recreation Park and there were many vendors' booths, of which the Green's Candies was one. Dorothy Engel was in charge of the booth and original team composed of one adult and two younger folks for each two-hour shifts. I would always work with the teams. We would coax one or both of the young folks to move into the crowds with a tray of assorted candies, coaxing the people to try some. As soon as they did this, the folks would invariably purchase some. The young folks seem to start out at the booths as introverts, but by the time they left they became extroverts. Some of the booth attendants were: Barb (Clonch) Durfey, the Green's Candies Queen until Jennifer Green came along, Susie Harmon (Wareham), Elizabeth (Burdis) Clark, Patty Durfey (Rule), and Karen Engle.

There were seven candy flavors: humbugs, molasses and peppermint flavor, which was formed as a rope and cut in opposite directions. All the rest were individual flavored anise, cherry, cinnamon, lemon, spearmint and sassafras. These were all packed up in 12-ounce trays, 4-ounce and 2-ounce bags, which had header labels. I also had a delicate tear drop jar. The jars were sealed with a red stretch tape and decorated with a red ribbon attached with green twist ties. Jen, Liz and Barb would pack candy in the cellar for the candy booth. They often referred to me as a slave driver. Profits from Green's Candies were donated to the hospital auxiliary.

We had quite a display booth. I had a large picture of my great-grandfather, Samuel Green, on the back wall, as well as other relatives involved over the past. Samuel Green was an un-ordained minister who brought the candy making art from Canterbury, England. He had a church in Fulton called Grace Chapel located on the street along the east side of the river just past Black Clawson. He had several ladies helping him for the children in Sunday school. Every fall, he would hold a banquet for all the newsboys in Fulton. It seemed like every boy in Fulton became a newsboy on that day so they could participate in the banquet. Today, Samuel Green's picture hangs at the Fulton Historical Society at the head of the stairs along with a smaller picture of my dad, Ray Green, in his by-plane.

My Uncle Harry and Aunt Bessie made the candy in the upstairs barn on their property across from the North End Paper Company on Hannibal Street. He also made ribbon candy, peanut brittle and various varieties of the delicious cream candies. It was in 1968 that we announced that we were starting to make the Green's candies. When we did, my Dad got several calls from ladies who worked with Samuel Green assisting him with church work. One of my dad's shirt-tailed relatives came to the house and demanded to be part of the enterprise and to share in the profits. Dad simply told him he was not entitled to it and that was the last we heard from him.

I had several customers that I was selling to. I would get up at 4am both Saturdays and Sundays, in the early months of the year, and work until 6:00pm. When I was ready to stop making it, it would take an hour to stop, clean up and put things away. I was doing well on my regular sales job and it was actually a good chance to unwind each week and rest up from the physical operation. My nephew, Dave Green, came one weekend to work with me. He couldn't get over how at 10am I would get tired, slow down the cooking, go into the front room and lay down flat on the rug for about 20 minutes, and then wake up totally revived.

My nephew, Dave Green, who at one time helped me make Green's Candies.

Eventually, I started to think about where I was going with this business in the future. No one in the family seemed to come forward expressing an interest in it. One of my customers told me there was a Board of Health man that came in and noticed I did not have an inspection number. I contacted him and he said he wanted to come in and inspect the operation before he issued one. At the time, I told him the operation was dismantled and put away. As it was, I ended up dumping about 800 pounds of product out back in the snow to dissolve, assuming it would not pass his inspection. When I told him what I had done, he told me, "You didn't have to do that." That was the end of my operation.

I have made small batches to give to family and friends. Since then, my grandson, Ryan, expressed an interest. I more or less discouraged him because of the liability factor. He was disappointed and so was I. It was too bad, but there are so many "sue-happy" people it wasn't worth the chance. In order to start up, it would take large amounts of cash to buy stainless steel equipment and a room equipped to handle this. I did offer everything I have, but he has since lost interest.

Chapter 10   Sandy

After I got home from my trip to Chicago to receive my president's award, our elderly neighbor, Mrs. Hazel Shaver (wife to Blanchard), set an evening for a neighborhood celebration. Each neighbor brought a dish to pass, did a lot of visiting and then Hazel called a moment to recognize me and my wife for my award achievement. Pictures were taken and congratulations made. It was a very nice get together.

Shortly after this, my wife passed away. Hazel set up a schedule: every Monday morning I was to go over to her house for a hearty breakfast, which I welcomed. She wanted to be sure I started the week out with a good meal. My good neighbors, Jim and Millie Durfey, had me over several times for a nice supper and friendly conversation. All of this helped me cope with my loss. Right after my wife passed away I took my son Tom, his wife Judy and family to the Thousand Islands for a nice outing, which included a relaxing boat ride. Judy had me stay at their house for a week so that I didn't have to stay at my house with all the memories. This worked out well for both families adjusting for the loss.

A few months later, my good friend Bob Kornbau (and wife Edna) was transferred to Bakersfield, California, as operations manager of Mobil Foams Plant which was next to the Bakersfield airport. I was invited out for a visit. Before I went, I pointed out to him that my lifestyle was a little different. I suggested that I would like to go to Las Vegas for a day or so. He told me that he had a travel agent, Sandra Helms, who he used and could set it up for me. Sandy was a travel agent for Kern Travel Agency in charge of the Bakersfield airport, where she handled Bob Kornbau's itinerary.

Edna and Bob Kornbau

The week I was scheduled to visit, I flew to Kansas City to a Flexographic Annual National meeting held. We had a good meeting with everyone. I remember Bill Bulmer our Canadian President was there. After the day's meeting, we went out barhopping and ended up at a lively one with a lot of ladies. So we didn't have any problem finding one to dance with. The next day I flew to Bakersfield to visit Bob via San Francisco. It was just sunset when we left Frisco on our way to Bakersfield. I was very impressed with the beautiful sunset view over the harbor.

After we settled into the flight, I struck up quite a conversation with a fine gentleman. We discussed many things. As it turned out, I later found out he was actually Sandy's boss at Kern's Travel in Bakersfield. After when he found out who I was, he advised Sandy to marry me. It turned out that his name was Tom Jarvis and his wife Dorothy ended up being our very good friends. They were very religious and had us over for many evening meals. He passed away but we kept in touch with his wife, until she became disabled and went to live with her son.

In fact, Bob invited Sandy to have dinner with all of us when I arrived. We all met and had a nice dinner at a very good steak house. Bob's wife, Edna, owned a Lincoln Town Car which we rode in. During the time there, Edna let me borrow this impressive auto. The days following, I started dating Sandra. After a day or so, she asked about her setting up a travel itinerary to Las Vegas. I had become quite impressed with her and told her I wouldn't go if I could continue to date her. She thought this was okay and we continued to date.

I used to pick her up at noon for lunch and evenings for dinner. Or she would invite me over to her house. She lived in her own residence at 1108 Westpoint Drive, Bakersfield. She was divorced from her husband, Bob Helms, but was dating one of Mobil Chemical Engineers who was divorced and had a son. He had been transferred to Mobil Chemical's Texas plant so he didn't get to see Sandy as often and not during the time I was visiting her.

One night, Sandy invited me over for a steak dinner at her house. Bob and Edna had their youngest son Garry living at home. I asked Garry to do me a favor and bring jewelry and flowers over during that evening meal as a surprise for Sandy, which he did. She seemed to be impressed. Eventually, time ran out on my stay and I flew back home to work. We kept in touch almost daily by phone, plus I sent her flowers daily.

As fall approached, I invited her to spend Thanksgiving with me in Fulton and she accepted. Before she arrived, I did some shopping for clothes with the help of a couple of waitress friends from Dubois Restaurant in Minetto, New York. Vince Caravan, my neighbor, used to go there Saturday nights with me. This is where I took Sandy for Thanksgiving dinner. I noticed her being in awe at all the trees and vegetation, even though they were dormant. This was quite a contrast to her home climate.

Sandy and I had become quite attached and I realized I would like to marry her and thought I had better propose to her while she was here and I had a chance. I left her at the house and went down to our local jewelers and purchased an engagement ring with the understanding that I could return it if things fell through. I brought the ring home and presented it to her and she accepted. We were both very happy about it! I did not introduce her to Tom's family.

His wife Judy said this would be best to do this after we were married. They did not want to be any influence on our decision.

Sandy flew back home and we continued our daily phone contact. We decided to set a date, Dec 17, 1977, to be married in California. She would then move here to Fulton. In the meantime, she made preparations to move here. She had her mother, Florence, and step-father, Chic Hutchins, move into her house in Bakersfield. This served two purposes: they would have a place to live and at the same time keep the place up for Sandy, who would also have a place to stay on visits. I flew out there in December and we were married on December 17.

We honeymooned in San Diego (Sandy had wanted to honeymoon in Hawaii but things didn't work out that way) and it was cloudy all the time we were there. We took a side trip to Tijuana, Mexico, and did some bartered shopping. She bought me an expensive leather belt with my name engraved on it. After our wedding, we made preparations to move her belongings to Fulton. It was a very stressful and emotional time for both Sandy and her mother, who was helping her. I remember loading the moving van which went along okay. Sandy had one particular box packed with different bottles of wine, etc. that she had accumulated on her trips with customers. The box of beverages was marked booze and I guess we were not surprised that it never made it to Fulton.

Chic, Sandy's stepfather, had a son Bob who was staying at her house and he moved out. Sandy had a Toyota Celica auto and we decided to have it sold by a friend in Bakersfield. Otherwise it would be very expensive to have it shipped. After she arrived here, we purchased her a Volkswagen Bug. This was very good in the snow.

In conversations over the phone with my daughter-in-law, Judy, she told me I had better make it back home for Christmas because the grandchildren expected our being there. As it was we had plane reservations to be back on December 24th, Christmas Eve, in Fulton. We boarded the plane in Bakersfield and looked out the window to wave goodbye to Sandy's mother, Florence Hutchins, who waved back but had a sad look on her face over Sandy's leaving. We arrived in Fulton Christmas Eve and went to Tom and Judy's on Christmas morning. Sandy met everyone and had a great time.

Right after the time when my wife Bea passed away, my daughter-in-law Judy, Tom's wife, invited me to come and sleep overnight for a week to help me adjust to the loss. This worked out very well. Unfortunately after I had married Sandy, Judy was afflicted with cancer that eventually took her life. I was at my Climax Manufacturing account when I got the call she was in the hospital. I came home and we waited for Nathaniel's bus to arrive and we took him to the hospital to see his mom. He was very close to his mother and had a difficult time understanding her passing.

Tom and his dad lived in their home with their Dalmatian pet dog. One particular day, when Tom had taken Nathanial to work with him at John M. Forester's, Tom got a call about a fire in his house and the troopers concerned that someone was in the house fire. It wasn't anyone but their pet dog that perished in the fire. Tom and Nate came to our house that night with only their shirts on their backs to stay with us until they could get their lives back together again with a permanent place to stay. Tom arranged for a trailer they could live in on a temporary basis while they had another house built.

Sandy kept working at a job placement company, Adecco Company, in Fulton. Don Unger was the manager and Bill Grace eventually came on board. Finally, the top management decided to close the Fulton branch, which was unusual because this office was most profitable of all the branches. They actually did Sandy a favor retiring her with a severance pay. She had been procrastinating on resigning anyway and was better off. Don was given retirement also and eventually bought a condo in Florida and moved there with his wife, Jeannie. The one remaining employee of the Fulton office was Bill Grace and he was transferred to Schoeller in Pulaski.

During our visit to California we took a side visit to Death Valley, where we visited Scotty's Castle. The place is an old hacienda that is self-sustained and now a national museum. There is a spring there used for drinking, cooling, etc. The story goes that an old prospector, Scotty, became friendly with a well-to-do engineer, Albert Johnson, out of San Francisco. Scotty persuaded the engineer to construct this elaborate compound. It had a musical room, reading room, etc. and had a large courtyard. There were very elaborate drapes made of small oval leather pieces stapled together hanging in several of the rooms. After that, we traveled back to Bakersfield and encountered heavy torrential rains. We made the trip back safely and were relieved.

One summer, Sandy arranged for my son and I to pick up a VW bus and tour Yellowstone. We entered through the west entrance and camped overnight at various campgrounds throughout the park. We fished for trout. They were very visible in the clear ponds. They appeared to be close to the surface when they were actually 10-15 feet down. One night after we were settled in, a ranger knocked at our door. He told us we had to move to a more secure campground because the bus had canvas sides where we had the roof expanded to accommodate one other person for sleeping area. I asked if we dropped the top down and locked it, could we stay. He said OK. I remember going to the back of the bus in the pitch dark to close it down and I experience goose bumps on the back of my neck, suspecting a bear. I hurried and got it locked down and went back inside. Fortunately, we had no bear visitors.

Chapter 11   The House on County Route 6

Eventually, we moved from Batavia Avenue to a home in the country on County Route 6. We decided to move and upgrade our home, plus Sandy was tired of some of the neighbors inadvertently reminding her of things that Bea did. A short time after we moved there, Ryan came to live with us taking up residence in our cellar.

Ryan always kept things going. He slept in our cellar. We had things set up for him down there. Seems like once a week I would go over to the school where something was going on and we talked to the teacher. All in all we got along pretty nice. One Sunday my wife and I took a ride. I come back home and here's my company car sitting by the road with a for sale sign. It was a brand new car that I had just picked up for use and Ryan had put the sign near it for a joke. There was a gentleman looking it over. And I was really infuriated with the fact that he inconvenienced somebody. I had to tell the guy that it wasn't for sale. Sandy and Ryan thought it was a funny thing. And it was.

We settled down in our new house enjoying the fireplace and outside view, etc. After moving in and getting more familiar with the house structure, we noticed several things that needed fixing. One was the house lacked caulking so I ended up using over ten tubes of caulk to close it up. We also noticed the clapboards, which were made of a synthetic composition, had a tendency to bow out around the structure. This was prevalent on the west side, where the sun hit it the most. As a result of these openings it served as a place for cluster flies to accumulate and eventually make their way into the two back bedrooms. My grandson and I went over the whole structure, using screws to draw the boards back in flush, thus eliminating the bows.

Later on, we noticed the inside walls on the corner north and west walls were showing separation. After examining possible causes, we discovered the attic did not have joists installed. After consulting with my brother-in-law, Hans, he drew up plans for joists to be installed. I hired a very good friend, Dave Bailey, shop instructor and housebuilder, to do this repair work. We purchased lumber from Burkes, a local lumberyard. We cut it properly and took them upstairs and fed them through the ceiling door opening to Dave. He actually completed the job in two days. He was a tireless worker.

After we were finished, we had the side of the house secured to avoid any problems. Later on, I decided to have an outside cellar entrance installed on the north end of the house. I hired a backhoe operator who dug this up with his machine. We cleared all the necessary dirt away, poured a slab and Dave laid up the blocks. We made the opening extra wide to accommodate the canoes I was building. We cut through the cellar walls with a cement saw and tied the cellar stairway walls to form a good seal. We finally installed a cellar door and a Bilco door for storm protection.

Ryan and I painted the house using scaffolding and ladders. On the north end, we used three tiers of scaffolding and an extension ladder to reach the third story high peak. At one point, the ladder on the top tier slipped off the baseboard that was warped and slid onto a solid flat board and held. We both experienced a good scare.

In order to reach out on the peak boards without having to move all the scaffolding, I taped my paintbrush to an old broom handle making it possible to reach out far enough. Later on, when the house needed a new coat of paint, Ryan, Cheryl and Duddy Rogers teamed up with us and got the job done. We were able to apply two coats of paint at the same time. We would apply the first coat over a given section and then go back to where we started and apply the second coat over it. The time we started over the first coat had set good enough. Over time, the paint has held up very well.

One time, we had a flooding in the cellar and there was no sump pump to handle this. There was an outside drain to handle this, but it was not working. I found the end of the outside drain line buried underground and blocked, holding the water back. I dug a trench and extended the drain line down and out far enough to let it come out on the side of the hill and I installed a cage over it. The drain has been working fine since.

Chapter 12 Camping & Other Recreational Activities

I recently learned about the state conservation taking ownership of the Gooli Club out of Glens Falls or Lake George area. The land and water was eight small lakes connected like the large chain lakes along Route 28 in the Old Forge Adirondack area. There were three routes to access the club's property. One was by Jeep out of Indian Lake following the Indian River to where the Cedar joins it, becoming the headwaters of the Hudson River. This is the location of the club's first camp used for hunting and stream fishing. We then traveled further into the third largest lake where the main camp was located on the bay. It consisted of a large main lodge used for cooking the meals for all the members. There were six or seven cabins used for groups of members or guests. Another access was by Jeep, entering through Newcomb off Route 28N. The third method was to fly in by float plane, usually taking off from Indian Lake for a 20-minute flight into the bay and main camp on the third lake.

I remember my first visit in with my dad and lawyer friend, Wilson Smith, using Winhauser's in a single engine float plane called a Cessna. We taxied out on the water, revved up the engines and headed to the far end of the lake. I could've sworn that he was going to run up on the further end of the lake. He tipped the nose of the plane to break the suction of the pontoons, allowing us to gain speed necessary. Then he really tipped the nose up and we were airborne. I was very impressed with the Cessna power and load carrying capacity.

An example of a Widgeon plane.

Another time, we flew in using Winhauser's Widgeon plane, with double overhead engines, and the main body riding in the water. We actually sat partway in the water. The day he came to pick us back out, it was very windy causing heavy white caps on the lake.

As we were taking off on the bay on our return trip, the pilot tilted the nose down to break the suction and overdid it, causing the nose to dip too far down, allowing water to come over the top of the plane. I panicked, jumped out of my seat and turned around to head for the overhead exit. As I did, I saw the looks on the red faces of the rest of the passengers and right then decided to turn back around and sit back down in my seat. I decided in that short time that, if they could take it, so could I. The pilot started out again and made a successful lift off.

Years later, I had the opportunity for another plane, this time with John Sharkey III, the owner of Universal Metals in Fulton. John took me out of Fulton to Watertown, then to Syracuse and came back to Fulton.

Getting ready for my plane ride with John Sharkey.

One time, we went in from Indian Lake and another time by auto out of the Newcomb entrance. Each party stayed in individual camps, sleeping there, and then getting up at 4:00am to the sound of the bell for breakfast in the main camp. Ella, the cook, and Byron, her husband and our guide, would make up lunches for the middle of the day. We would always come ashore at noon by this large rock where there was a spring. Byron started a small fire and we toasted our sandwiches over it. It was like a gourmet lunch! We usually trolled until 4 pm and went back to camp for our evening meal. We trolled using a combination lure and minnow. When we didn't have any luck catching anything, Byron would say, "Well, we had better have a beer to get the fish to bite."

The main fish caught were lake trout and an occasional brook trout. My dad always hired Byron as a guide on the first day of fishing. On one weekend, it was decided that he would take us across the lake and hike into a good trout stream. He carried a back basket carrying our lunches, etc. We unloaded across the lake and started up over a hill, coming to a very large spring containing many fingerling trout. This was a puzzle to me as to how the trout got up there above the level of the lake. We went on, arriving at the stream that was fairly wide and full of moving water. We came across a beaver dam that crossed the stream. Just then, there was a mother wood duck traveling upstream with all her ducklings. When she got to the dam, she flew over it and landed on the upper side of it. We stood there in awe watching all of this. Just then, the ducklings all wove their way up the branches of the dam coming out on top, and joined their mother.

When the excitement calmed down, we started stream fishing with very good luck catching good-sized native brook trout. We could actually see them in the very deep clear water. In the evenings after supper, everyone would retire to their cabins for the night. Byron would come around, paying a visit to each cabin, joining them all in a cocktail. By the time he completed his stops, he wasn't feeling any pain.

On one weekend, my dad and Winfred visited the Gooli Club for a holiday. Winifred had a way of working on Dad's nerves and upsetting him. This was happening to the point that he developed hiccups and was unable to stop them. They had to drive him out to the doctors on a Sunday. The doctor froze his stomach somehow to cure him. The Gooli Club was his only means of getting away from Winifred to he could relax enough to face her for another week's time.

On another occasion when driving in to the club on a rough road, we hit a rock puncturing the oil pan. In order to stop the leak, Byron used bread, poking it into the hole, letting it swell and thus plugging the hole. This enabled them to drive home and get a new oil pan. I have never heard of this technique of using the bread.

After Dad passed away, that ended my trips to the club. I was offered to take over his membership, but I couldn't afford it. I really missed going there. I hope to pay a visit under the state ownership open to the public.

My first snowmobile was a 1968 Scorpion, 18 horsepower with Sacs powered engine. It ran very well, but in order to steer it, I used to stand up on the running boards and lean forward, putting my weight on the skis, making it turn effectively. I used to get a good workout in the fields behind the house. I would actually break out in a good sweat. I made up a triangular tow bar hooked onto the front of my toboggan so I could give the kids a ride.

I had some mechanical problems with the snowmobile. A drive chain would break and I would have just about twenty minutes to work on it before the parts became very cold. I used to have to add linkage to the chain to fix it. After a while, I was able to get a heavier chain that held up much better. I built a four-inch-high compartment under the full length of the seat so I could store parts and tools to work on it during breakdowns out in the field. There were times when I would get stuck in the fluffy snow in the fields. When I got off the machine to free it, I would end up in snow up to my hips. In order to get going, I would wade in the snow in front of the machine so I could get back on and go. Some of the times, on an extended trip, I would tie snowshoes, one on each side so in case I couldn't drive out of the field, I could snowshoe out.

On one occasion, I took it to Old Forge for the weekend to meet with customers from the Rochester area. We drove over 125 miles on that weekend through the woods and over frozen lakes. On one stop, I had to get a tool out from under the seat. My customer saw the open area with all my tools and parts and asked me if I had any tools left home. The following weekend, I had it parked out back and one of my neighbor's rode it because we were going away. When I got back, I saw it in the field. A shaft had broken and I had to tow it back in and get it repaired at a shop. I couldn't help realize how close I came to having this happen to me while up north out in the wilderness.

We had agreed to meet at the Back Door Bar of Howard Johnson's in Old Forge and then go on to stay at their friend's camp further on. I arrived there after they did, gulped down a drink and then ordered another one. My friend, Don said, "Gee Bob, you are drinking fast." I said, "Well, I was trying to catch up with them." He said they had just gotten there a few minutes earlier and were still on their first drink. The next day, it was raining and we had to drive our machines the back way into Old Forge to purchase our trail permits. The riding wasn't that great, but the weather got colder, making it better snow riding. The day we were to come home, we had trouble getting our vehicles out of the lower part of the driveway because the rain had frozen, making it very slippery. My two friends tied on to each vehicle with snowmobiles and pulled us out of there. They were slipping and sliding, but they pulled us out of there.

I eventually purchased an Arctic Cat, a one-person machine, and later on, a 1977 Panther Artic Cat. At the time our grandson, Ryan, lived with us and he used to drive Panther all over. One Sunday afternoon he called me while I had a bad cold and cough. He told me, "Gramps you are not going to like this." I told him, I didn't think so either. He had come over the top of a hill and not being able to stop, ran directly into a creek. As it was, one ski was hung up on the ice holding the whole machine from going under.

I had a dodge pickup truck, which I parked up the hill from the machine facing road traffic (wrong side of the road). I had waders on and was able to tie onto the machine with a rope that went up around a post and attached to the back of the truck. I had Jennifer drive ahead and pull the machine out. We got it up out of the water and into the truck and took it on home. Later I took it to a serviceman who specialized in electronics and he was able to fix it. Everything turned out alright. As I saw my youngest grandson, Nate, growing up, I decided to sell both machines to avoid any future problems. He was disappointed.

A while after Sandy came here from California, we took a trip up to Old Forge to snowmobile with my two snowmobiles. Sandy had never been on one before. She was driving my Panther Arctic Cat, following me with my Cheetah Arctic Cat. I kept checking back to make sure she was keeping up. One time I looked back, she wasn't following me, so I pulled over and waited. She didn't show up so I went back to check on her and she was on the machine. She had caught a small sapling between her skis on a turn. She was in a panic situation. I apologized to calm her down and got the snowmobile back on the trail. She continued on with me to our destination.

One summer day in the Adirondacks, my two grandsons, Ryan and Nate, along with Lance Durfey, were swimming at Rawlins Pond. It was a very hot day after we got through drying off I got in our car's driver's seat and pulled the sun visor down to keep the sun out of my eyes. Just as I did, a large Hershey bar that I stored there, slid down onto my bare chest, coating me with hot syrupy chocolate that had melted in the hot sun. I was screaming bloody murder as I was trying to wipe it off. All the boys did was get a good laugh out of the situation. It was a very funny scene to them. I finally cleaned myself off, and as I did, the chocolate cooled down to a more tolerable temperature. Eventually, we all had a good laugh over it.

My brother, Gerald, and wife, Betty, would always spend a weekend at Firemen's Field Days in Old Forge. Sandy and I joined them and their farming friends from Moravia. Gerald and I would get up early and cook breakfast for the group: bacon, eggs, pancakes and home fries. We had our own "real" maple syrup that we shared. During the day, we would go into town and sometimes have lunch at Gerald's favorite, Stickler's Diner. We would also go to Walt's Diner for an early morning coffee. The diner's owner passed away and his wife took over cooking. She would get frustrated being behind on her cooking. She would lock the front door until she caught up and then reopen. It was an amusing time for us to watch in good humor.

Saturday evening we would have our cocktail hour and Gerald would cook steaks for all. We also had home fries, beans, and corn on the cob. Eventually, the grandchildren would join us at different camps we stayed at. One weekend, we stayed at Winslow's, a large hotel on Third Lake, which was sort of rundown. One night, we had thunderstorms and the lights went out. The boathouse had a nice coat of paint, but the roof had caved in. The groundskeeper was a little slow at getting his maintenance done. One time, Nate and his friends stopped by from their camp and we had a good time, but they were getting into our beer and becoming quite loud and fouled mouth. Eventually, I suggested they go back to their camp.

One time, during the day, they went out on a lake in two of my cedar strip canoes and hung out talking about whatever. I took a picture of Ryan and Sandy standing by my 16-foot cedar strip cottage canoe. It was a good picture of the canoe showing the light and dark bands of the wood. I have since passed this on, plus the homemade paddles, to Russell, Jennifer and family. Jennifer wanted to make sure she got this one especially.

Eventually, we started camping at Eagle Bay Village, which had several camps and a large new single house. The young folks eventually took over the menus and replaced the steak with Italian dishes. This was all much more efficient, but disappointing to Gerald and I. On the last weekend of the year, Gerald was still with us and I cooked our own meals on Saturday night. Sandy and I had steak. After we joined the group at the large camp, Gerald said to me, "I heard you had steaks." I felt bad not to have included one for him.

At the end of the fishing party boat activities, we would go back to

I'm on the right. My brother Gerald is on my left and his two sons, Bob and David, are behind us.

our cabins and cook the evening meal which consisted of steak, beans, corn on the cob, salad, etc. Lance would stay around the campfire with us. His trip was Tupper Lake, Blue Mountain, Long Lake, and Raquette Lake.

Way back when I was still living at 212 Batavia Avenue, Fulton, Jim Durfey, Dick Gordon, Lee Sheldon and I would always do a weekend fishing-camping trip to Stillwater in the spring and fall. We set up camp in a triangle area where the Sunday Creek ran into Twitchell Creek. We used Jim Durfey's tent trailer that got us up off the ground.

Once, after I had purchased a Chevrolet Suburban, we used it to pull the trailer and have all of our gear stored here. I remember the first weekend trip with the Suburban. I was riding in the back seat with Dick Gordon, our southern friend. He looked over everything, outside down to the ground, he turned to me and said,

"This is like riding a chariot." When we got to our destination I proceeded to park the trailer on the site. At one point, I got out of the Suburban to walk around and check our position. I then got back into the vehicle to finish up. After I got back in, I said "where is the steering wheel?" and realized I was in the back seat. This was because the vehicle was longer than a car and I did not look up to see where I was going. We all had a good laugh about it.

We got settled, started a fire and Dick would usually cook the meal. At one evening meal time, Jim was cooking our steaks and dropped one in the sand. We washed it all off and he made sure he got that one. Jim couldn't get over the fact that everyone thought they got the one that was dropped. After supper we would play cards, have limburger cheese and crackers. Everyone was forced to join in or get all choked up with the smell of limburger. We all had a good time. Lee and Dick usually caught the most trout, with Jim coming in third, and me last.

In recent years, I have been doing canoe presentations on Thursday afternoons in the fall at Selkirk on Oswego County Soil & Water Conservation Day program for around 500 fifth grade students. I have been able to do this with the assistance of Don Ross and, of recent years, Doug Blake. This schedule always fell on the Green's fall reunion. This caused me to miss one day, Thursday, of it. We used to have real good times with nieces and nephews coming from quite a way away. Hans and Edith used to join us as well.

My Adirondack guide boat. My great-grandson, Nick, helped me at the Selkirk event.

As of this year, the event has fizzled out. Grandson Ryan and wife Cheryl are staying in their own tent camper at Nick's Lake, while Sandy and I are staying at Christie's hotel in Old Forge. At this time, I hope we can get together. Other times, we would rent a party boat on Raquette Lake and troll up the Marion River, pull into the old spring hole and still fish. We would light up a cigar, have a beer and totally relax. For years, I would invite my former neighbor and fishing partner, Lance Durfey, from Tupper Lake.

On one weekend in the spring, my neighbor Jim Durfey, his tenant

Al Hartman, friends, Lee Sheldon, Dick Gordon and I decided to go to Stillwater Reservoir for our annual spring weekend camping and trout fishing. This happened to be Al's first day going to the ADK and of course he was all excited and looking forward to it. He owned a pickup slide on camper which he took along. What we neglected to tell Al was all about the black flies which would be a problem.

On an early Saturday morning, we had breakfast and all took off for different sections of the stream. (Twitchell Creek, which flows out of Twitchell Lake down into Stillwater Reservoir.) We hoped to catch our limit of trout. No more than two hours went by when Al went back to the camper to get away from all the pesky black flies. On his way up out of the stream he passed me cursing and saying to me, "You call this FUN, Green"?

Later on, he and I took Jim's wooden boat which he built and along with my dad's three-horsepower Johnson outboard motor. We did some trolling where we were away from the black flies. As we were moving along, I opened the motor gas cap to see that it needed more gas. So, like a jerk I proceeded to top it off with our gas supply can. No sooner had I started, some of the gas ran down the side of the motor and immediately caught on fire, including my pants. I immediately jumped overboard, extinguishing the flames on my pants.

I came up to the surface with Al sitting dumbfounded looking at the motor and surrounding flames. I hollered to him to put the fire out as I climbed out of the water to help. Needless to say, water got into the gas tank and I ended up rowing back to the car and trailer on shore. We loaded the boat on the trailer and headed back to camp. On the way back, I suggested to Al that we keep the incident to ourselves and he agreed.

My grandchildren and greatgrandchildren. Top left: Jennifer and Russel's wedding. Bottom left: Jennifer, Russell, Garret and Julian. Top right: Cheryl and Ryan. Bottom right: Nate, Robin and Nick.

Chapter 13   Woodworking

One time, while working in the machine shop, I decided to build a set of skis between work projects. I worked with a carpenter and build the basic skis extra-long. My thought was that longer skis would give me extra balance. The next step was to bend the tip of the skis for breaking through the snow. The blacksmith, Mel Taylor, came up with the idea of soaking the front end of the skis in the water barrel overnight to soften the wood. In the meantime, Mel fashioned tips out of iron by heating them in his forge and then bend them while they were red hot and dipped them in cold water to temper the wood.

As soon as the skis soaked overnight, Mel heated the metal molds one by one and clamped the ski tips over them. Because the moisture in the wood would turn to steam, softening the wood fibers and allowing them to conform to the metal forms. Next, I took sections out of discarded thick leather belts and fashioned foot pads and glued them in the center of the skis. I made leather straps for my feet. I found it was difficult for me to control the skis, keeping them straight in a line down the hill. The problem with this is that it was caused by the lack of long grooves in the bottom of the skis. This didn't register with me and the skis ended up being runners for the snow sled we made for ice fishing, end of story.

In regards to boat building, I have completed six of them and am working on a seventh, which is a 14-foot guide boat. I have laminated the ribs and attached them to the bottom board. I plan to plank the hull the original way the old timers used to. This last one has been on hold at this stage for over four years. I hope to get at it soon.

The first canoe was called a "Laker," built from plans out of a *Popular Mechanics* magazine. This was a very stable canoe. I used to attach a side motor mount and mount my dad's three-horsepower gas Johnson motor. I used it on Stillwater with Jim Durfey on our fishing weekend. In the fall, I stored it upside down on the strong-back. Unbeknownst to me, over the winter the snow dumped on it and in the spring it was thawing and freezing, it got crushed beyond salvaging. I built a second one from the same plans as the first one. Nate helped me do some of the stripping, but eventually lost interest. So I finished it up alone. This one handles very well as compared to the first one. I never put a motor on it because I was reluctant to put the license number on it.

The third canoe was called a "Peterborough," a cottage canoe. This one was 16 feet, but a little narrower than the "Laker." It was a sleeker-looking craft. As I built it, I ended up grouping strips that were darker in the same matching order on both sides. The decks were fancier and the gunnels were chestnut, which I had to scarf or splice to make up the length on either side. I have since passed this canoe and a set of paddles I made to Ross and Jen. They were very pleased to receive it, as I was giving it. It will come in handy as a showpiece and if they use it on Lake George. It is a one-of-a-kind boat for them to remember me by.

The fourth and fifth cedar strip canoes are called a "Wee Vera," a more streamlined craft, a modified version of "Rushton's Wee Lassie." He was a well-known canoe builder in Canton, New York. These are 10 foot 4 inches in length and the decks are considerably longer. One has a conventional woven cane seat and the other has a woven rawhide seat.

This was my first attempt at rawhide weaving. When looking for a source, I called a supplier in Wisconsin and he asked me what I was going to use it for. When I told him, he replied that he would want some thicker material from the hindquarters of a pig. This worked out very well.

I also made an accent strip out of dark cedar and lighter basswood and placed it on both sides two or three inches down from the gunnels, giving the canoe a nice touch. The decks were made of strips alternating of cherry and basswood. The cowling face of the decks was made of two thin layers of cherry, laminated. The gunnels were made of spruce having a thin outer layer of cherry hardwood laminated to it, thus giving the gunnels more protection. The thwarts seat backs were made of cherry strips laminated and fiberglass/antipoxy.

All of these canoes were covered inside and out with fiberglass and epoxy coating. The inside had two coats of epoxy, leaving a mesh pattern to prevent slipping. The outside had three coats of epoxy. Both inside and out had three coats of a UV varnish to protect the epoxy from becoming brittle from the sun's rays.

Instructions in the *Popular Mechanics* did not call for UV varnish and this could have contributed to the first canoe becoming brittle and crushing. I put one of these canoes in a neighbor's pool to see how it floated. This was before I had put in the seats and thwarts. I took a picture of Ryan laying in it and Cheryl sitting on the edge of the pool.

These two short 10 foot 4 inch canoes were built using a strong back and framing given to me by a fellow canoe builder, Steve Lunn. The first of these two is hanging up on display in the outside bar at the Tavern on the Lock. It is due to be brought home soon. A special sign describing the story of it hangs under it.

As for my first 16-foot guide boat, it took me ten months to build using the laminated ribs and cedar strip construction. This is a replica of a 1905 Virginia model. Everything was built from scratch including a pair of 8-foot oars. The plans and instructions were from a book, "Building an Adirondack Guide Boat: Wood Strip Reproductions of the Virginia Paperback," by Michael J. Olivette and John D. Michne.

The authors warned that the project was not to be attempted by a novice. They were so right. The original guide boats were like the pickup truck of the Adirondacks. The plans call for laminated spruce ribs and cedar strip planking, cherry decks gunnels and thwarts and seats. The outside was epoxy, coated in the same manner as the cedar strip canoes. The outside bow and stern contained ¼-inch brass strip, or bang plate. The same brass strips were applied in three strips on the bottom, giving the hull very good protection when beaching it. The ribs in the original boats were made from spruce stumps. The builder would dig up the stumps, clean them and cut them in 4-inch thick pieces. They cured them two years and cut four ribs out at a time using their precut patterns.

After they were cured, they would rip 4-inch individual ribs from the 4-inch slab. Each individual rib was actually half a rib, so they would end up attaching the ribs to the bottom board. There were usually 64 ribs in a 16-foot boat. They were secured on an accurately built jig that was securely braced. They used brass screws and copper tacks that were clenched over. They would use a composite made of lead and varnish to seal the seams. Today, they use a bedding compound that would remain pliable in its original form. Usually when they put the boats in the water they would leak, so they would submerge them for a couple of days letting it swell and seal the leaks.

The oars were 8-foot long, requiring one to cross hands and give the oars extra effortless, thrust propelling the boat at a good speed. On this latest 14-foot boat, I plan to use cedar and plank the hull, making it the traditional way. I'll probably fiberglass/epoxy the outside and UV varnish the same as the 16-foot cedar strip original guide boat I built. I also have two other Old Town canoes that I restored. I expect to sell them outright. One is a 1952 13-foot Old Town trapper model red in color. When I acquired it, 13 of the ribs were broken and the hull was caved in. In order to get it back to its original length and shape, I had to steam it, cover the sides with canvas and trim it with heavy shears. The other is a 16-foot Sixtieth Anniversary model Molitar painted white.

Chapter 14   Trip to Ohio

Sandy and I traveled to Sharon Center, Ohio, to visit our niece Ella and nephew Ken Raw. Got up 4:00am Sunday to pack and had breakfast and left at 7:00am. I drove one and a half hours until just past Rochester on the Thruway. We took a break there and Sandy drove the rest of the way. Our niece Ella supplied us with very good instructions, with us arriving at 2:30 pm, in 7.5 hours. We were all very happy to see each other, unloaded and went into their excellent accommodations. We had the entire upstairs consisting of two bedrooms and a full bath. We went out to dinner at Bob Evans Farm Restaurant. Monday, we visited their daughter, Joy Molner's real estate business where both couples worked.

We visited Lehman's store, an old-fashioned hardware in Dalton, Ohio. We had a hearty lunch there and then toured the facility. They handled all kinds of products not usually found in a hardware store. I found handle parts for a two-man cross cut saw that I had been looking for to replace the one missing on mine.

After that, we visited Smucker's jelly store and picked up some unusual flavors of jelly, etc. That evening we had a family reunion at Ken and Ella's. Her three brothers came, Ken and his wife, Kris alone, and Karl and his wife. We had a fun time reminiscing about the good old days.

Ella, Sandy and I went to breakfast at Valley Buffet in Wadsworth, everyone but I had a nice breakfast. I ordered hash and their famous home fries and I could hardly eat them. I told the waitress I felt bad that I could not finish the food and felt bad for the dog they would give it to. The waitress took it off the bill.

We visited Ella and Dave Molner's home that morning. We visited a large bulk food store, Sherry's in Fredericksburg, Pennsylvania, where we purchased a lot of exotic foods. We went on to Keim Lumber Company in Charm, Ohio. They handled many exotic woods from Africa and South America and they also handled many hard to find wood working tools. Later, we had dinner at a family style Amish restaurant. We went back to Ken and Ella's and went to bed.

We went to visit Ken and Ella's son and daughter-in-law, Rob and Candice Raw. Their son, Max, aged seven, and his dad just came back from the dentist. Rob had brought home some sandwiches from Panera. We toured their home and had a nice visit. After that we all went to a tourist railroad station for our lunch. Unfortunately the train was not running during our time there. Ella, Sandy and I went back to Ella's house, while Ken went with Rob's family to do some other activities. After Ken came home, we all went to Medina to have supper there at a place called Dan's Dog, famous for its old-fashioned atmosphere and its special hot dogs. We were joined there by Dave and Joy Molner, their daughter Morgan and a friend. It was crowded and noisy but had a good atmosphere.

The next day, we had blueberry pancakes for breakfast. Ken Raw and I visited his cousins to view his miniature toy collection that he builds as a hobby. I was able to purchase a dark walnut plank to be used in my stool building projects. We went back to the house and enjoyed corn chowder. Later on, we went to Hartsville and met my niece Beth Guzzmann and her husband for dinner. We evaluated and identified family photographs.

Chapter 15   Ryan

Ryan had a job at the Lock, working in the restaurant. I guess he used to do dishes downstairs as part of his duties. One night, he was pulling dishes out of the dumbwaiter and the door came down and hit him on the back of his neck. He said he saw stars, but he got over it OK. I don't know how long after that, but he had problems with his left arm and cold-like symptoms. He went to the doctor and he said he had a brain stem tumor, they thought. They set it up and he was sent to Syracuse and they were treating him for cancer.

The doctors didn't really know how to cure him and he just kept getting worse and worse. I was very frustrated as the rest of us were, trying to find a way to help Ryan. Every night I would pray that something would come to help him. Lo and behold, one night I was reading a *Reader's Digest* with an article called, "What's Happened to Fred?" At the end of the article, it said he was the guy who perfected brain stem and spinal cell tumor removal. So I got the number for this doctor, Dr. Fred J. Epstein, through my factory out of Linden. I called this gentleman up and I told his secretary what was going on with Ryan. She said to send the MRI down and Dr. Epstein would look at it and get back to me.

I went to the Syracuse hospital and got a copy of the MRI. I was very nervous doing that because I was afraid the doctor would hear and get annoyed and not treat Ryan. But that didn't happen. So I sent it down to Dr. Epstein and, lo and behold, he called me on a Friday to say he was in Florida on his vacation, but would call me back. He did and we discussed the situation. Dr. Epstein said it was definitely operable, which was really good news. I asked, "Can you do it?" and he said, "Of course, I do it all the time." "I beg your pardon," I said, "I meant *will* you do it?" He said "Why certainly. Call my secretary to set up an appointment and we'll get it done."

I told the doctor that we would like to have a consultation first, if he didn't mind because Ryan was kind of nervous about the whole thing. The doctor said that was OK, and we set up a time to go to New York. We made arrangements by airplane and that worked out fine. Ryan and his dad flew down there and I took the train and met them. We went to the hospital and talked to the doctor.

After we acquired Dr. Fred Epstein, Ryan, his dad and I took the train to New York City and went to his office, which is not too far from the train station. We had an interview with him as I started to say before, we had a conference and were trying to decide whether he should operate or not. He made the decision for us, stating it was definitely operable. We set up a time for the operation and took the train back home that same day. Later on, Dr. Epstein made an appointment to do the operation.

Ryan and his dad flew down in a private jet that his dad was able to get passage on. We don't know who the company was; it was certainly a nice deal. Cheryl, Ryan's girlfriend, and I took the train down. We ended up staying at the Ronald McDonald House in New York City. The three of us were all in one room for the night and we all got along very well. It certainly saved us a lot of money. It was something to see the different people who were staying there. They were from all over the world.

We arrived at the hospital and got ready. They took Ryan for his operation down on the elevator and we sure were reluctant to let him go, but the team assured us he would be OK and they would take care of him. We waited in the waiting room. In the meantime, other doctors that operated there would come in and have meetings with the families of other patients about their outcomes. Some were good and some were bad.

After quite some time, they finally came out and told us that they had to pull back on the operation. What they had done, was put the probe in to monitor the heart. They had never experienced Ryan's increase in heartbeat with other young people before, and very few older people. So they had to pull back and put him under a heart surgeon's care, which went over the weekend. So we just waited.

They took him in Monday. They did the operation and it was successful.

We had to wait for him to recover to take him home. We spent 16 days total. In the meantime, Cheryl had to get back to school, so she went back ahead of time, once she knew everything was OK. I give her a lot of credit for sticking with it. A lot of other gals would have just walked away. She was in love with Ryan and stuck with him. We are all thankful for that.

In the meantime, Ryan was in his bed, he had a photo of his heart when they stuck the probe in to check his heartbeat and he put it up on the window overlooking the East River. The nurse came in and said "What's this doing up here? You ought to take that down." Ryan said "No, leave it up. I got it there so I can show my friends when they come in." So she left it up there. I guess this was before the operation.

We had all this time to stay with him, to keep him company and we would go back to the Ronald McDonald House at night and so forth. That was our ritual. While he was recovering there was a pair of lawyers came in and wanted to sue the Syracuse Hospital for malpractice. They apparently had enough evidence, I don't know. Ryan and his dad thought it was a good idea. I kind of talked them out of it because it would have subjected Dr. Epstein's time at a trial which would be robbing other people of his services. So we just kind of let that go.

When it came time to go back home, Ryan's dad got hold of the people that had the flight for us and they allowed me to ride back with them to Rochester. We went to White Plains where they drove us by car, to the airplane and flew us into Rochester. Sandy drove up to the airplane to pick us up and brought us home.

Before that Ryan was very skeptical, which is normal after an operation like that, that he would be able to get downstairs to the car and all that. I assured him we would make it OK . We went very slowly and we did it OK, no mishap.

After Ryan recovered, he went back to work at the Sealright Company, which later became Huhtamaki. So I went to visit a friend in charge of manufacturing and he assured us that Ryan had his job, which worked out fine with everybody. Ryan was on the verge of being handicapped or OK; he chose to go back to work. I am very proud of him for making that decision. He is still working today.

Dr. Epstein has written a book called the "Gifts of Time," a story about a pioneering surgeon and the children who were his mission. He is dedicated to saving children. I bought two copies of that and had him sign one of them. Ryan ended up with that one. It's a very educational and inspiring book to read.

The doctor told us that he used Ryan's operation as a subject in the classes that he taught in a college down there for would-be-doctors. That was quite a nice thing. Ryan's dad, Tom, deserves a lot of credit for his part in procuring the transportation down and back. I don't know how he did it, but he did a great job and saved us a lot of monkeying around.

Eventually Ryan and his girl were married, which we were very pleased about. They had each other to take care of; they will have a happy life together.

Ryan went to St. Camillus for rehab and about two or three months later, while he was still recovering, I had the opportunity to take my motorhome out to Breckenridge, Colorado to deliver it to Doug Caster's brother. Doug negotiated the sale for his brother with me. He took care of all the gas going out and the return flight in the air.

We had a very nice trip out and stopped in Ohio to visit my sister on the way. We went to the air museum on the way out. We would find a campground along the way, pull in and stay overnight. When we got out west, we started going to the forts out there. They were historic, but they ended up being just like cities. Because of that, Ryan said: "What do you say we don't go to any more of those." So we didn't.

On our way out, we were fascinated. As we headed towards the mountains it was flat all the way. Then, all of the sudden, mountains were rolling up. We got into Denver, Colorado, about 4:30 in the afternoon. I made the wrong turn with the motorhome and we ended up in Coors' parking lot. One of the officials was coming out of the building and I asked him how to get back onto the highway. He gave us instructions and after we found our way back, we stayed overnight in the city park. It was like being up in the Adirondacks, it was so primitive. The next morning, we took off and went up to Breckenridge to see the place Mr. Caster had reserved for us.

I guess Breckenridge is about 7,000 to 8,000 feet above sea level and I didn't pay attention to it. We pulled in, got out of the motorhome and I felt totally exhausted, like you are after a long trip. It didn't seem to go away right away, which I guess was because of the lack of oxygen that high up. Eventually, we got accustomed to it.

We rented Arctic Cat snowmobiles at Copper Mountain and were advised to wear sunglasses and sunscreen. We thought we were tough and didn't have to do that, so we did not heed the advice. The sun was so bright it was hard to see the variations in the hills and valleys, but we did OK. Not realizing how intense the sun was at that elevation, we paid for it in the end with a bad sunburn. We went up to an area overlooking an area called 'Climax' where the troops would train on skis and so forth. It was quite a sight, you could see way down, see their facility down there.

After we got done, Ryan was pleased with himself that he could handle the snowmobile so soon after his surgery. We came back and spent a few days there until it was time to go back. I think we went to Golden to do a little gambling. We didn't spend too much money.

Another day we went up to Leadville, a very famous town in the old days for gold. John Wayne made a movie there. We went to the National Fish Hatchery on a Saturday; they were closed, but we got to see part of it. The streams were going across one of the roads. I would have liked to have gone back there and do some stream fishing, but I never did. While we were going over to Leadville, we were on this route where on the passenger's side it went straight down. Ryan said "Get over, you are getting too close!" but I was right where I belonged in the road. It was pretty scary for him. Me, too!

On the morning we were to take off and go back to the airport, we were to be picked up by a limousine. It was snowing pretty heavy, but it was the springtime of the year for them. It was a different snow. I was wondering how we were going to get down to the airport on time. But they picked us up and took us back down. When we got to around 5,000 feet elevation, it turned to rain. That was really surprising.

We got to the airport, took our flight back and ended up in the Newark, New Jersey airport to catch another flight back home. I was making a phone call in the airport in Newark and apparently somebody somehow got my credit card number. After that trip, the phone company called me and asked if I was making calls to Beirut and places like that. I said no. They changed my number and it didn't cost me anything. That's how easily people can get your number.

Ryan got practice using the tractor, wandering around. Later on he was right on the spot if I happen to mention anything I would be doing, he'd be right there to help me on it. He is quite a nice grandson. We think the world of him and Cheryl.

Dr. Epstein was a very well-known surgeon. As I said, he is mainly interested in operating and saving children's lives, which he did. He was on TV several times. Part of it is that he taught his procedure in classes at the Tisch Hospital in New York City. But ironically, he fell off while riding his bicycle one time and injured his head. Eventually he died from those injuries, which is a sad situation. At least his procedures were taught to other people to carry it on.

In the meantime, before he died, one of the hospitals built a special wing for him and another doctor that did internal medicine. It was family-friendly so the families could come there and stay while their family member was being operated on which made it a lot less stressful, which is a nice thing.

After Ryan's operation, he was assigned to St. Camillus for rehab. I would take him up every day for therapy. He was very slow to begin with, which is normal. He finally got therapy where he could move, and recovered. After that was done they recommended he get into an exercise routine. So I went to the

Fulton YMCA and talked to the director, who allowed Ryan to go there, and myself, without any fee for about a three-month period of time. That's how we carried his therapy on even further. We were quite grateful for that. Vince Caravan, my former neighbor, wrote Ryan's story, and published it in his paper. Vince was always good about those things.

Chapter 16   Sandy's Operation

Over time, Sandy developed chronic back and leg pains caused by the deterioration of her vertebrae. We ended up taking her to a specialist who recommended two operations. The first was for the neck. The purpose of that was to shorten up the amount of time she would have to be on the operating table, face down. In the neck operation, they went through the front of her neck and replaced four vertebrae. She had to wear a neck brace for thirty days as well as having electric stimulators attached to both sides of her neck. The purpose of these was to promote bone growth over the replaced vertebrae.

The result of the operation and electric stimulators were successful in relieving the pain, but three weeks after the operation she suddenly became deaf in her right ear. She visited the Ear, Nose and Throat Doctor to discuss this loss and the doctor said she would not get that hearing back.

Since then, she hears dial tones in her right ear. She visited another specialist, who recommended her to continue a certain medicine to hopefully get the hearing back.

After she has healed from the neck operation, she may be scheduled for the back operation. That decision will be made depending on if her hearing comes back.

Chapter 17   Community Service

After my retirement, a group of us, we called ourselves the 'lunch bunch,' started going out to lunch at RFH's on Wednesdays and sometimes went to Weedsport Family Diner, where they had excellent pies. Some of the people were Lorry Rogers, Bart Chalone, Art Jones, Don Ross, Morris Sorbello, Wally Auser, Fran Mirabito and Vince Caravan and Brenda Niver, who was our token "broad." Eventually, the group was reduced to just myself, Don Ross, Fran Mirabito with Brenda, meeting at Tavern on the Lock. Friday noons, Vince, Sherry Hillick, Art Jones, Dave, Ryan and I would go to the Lock for lunch.

During these times, Vince and I used to meet on Mondays at Mimi's. I always enjoyed their chipped beef on toast. Don Ross and I would always meet at noon at the Blue Moon. Occasionally Morris and the Universal Metal people, John Starkey III and John Starkey IV, the latter took charge of the full business operation. Recently John III took me for a nice airplane ride from Fulton to

Watertown to Syracuse and back to Fulton. This was good practice for him and an enjoyable ride for me. He was a very gracious host.

I was a member of IMC (Industrial Management Club). Their purpose was to promote management skills, etc. and we would meet in the evening. Eventually, I was invited to become their president for a year. We would invite different guest speakers with appropriate skills that would be a benefit to us. After my term, I stayed on acting as their pastor and eventually resigned. It was always a challenge to find a suitable prayer.

I recently had the privilege along with Vince Caravan and Keith Baker to take the World War II honor flight out of Rochester to Washington, D.C., to visit the WW II memorials. Each one of us was assigned a volunteer civilian escort for the entire trip. We stayed overnight in Rochester and got up at 4:00am and assembled with the rest of the veterans at the airport in Rochester for the trip. I was very impressed with the variety of people seeing us off. Some were civilians and some were in full uniform.

On our return trip we were very surprised with the reception at the airport. There were relatives of the servicemen and also military personnel in full uniform. They were lined up on both sides as we walked along to the reception planned for us. There were several children on each side waving and thanking us for our service. I made it a point to shake hands with all the children I could. On our way home, Vince was so thankful that we stayed for the ceremony. We were all very humbled and thankful for this opportunity.

Along the way, Erica Schreiner, the of Oswego County Soil & Water, had invited me to Selkirk State Park for their Fall Conservation Day. She had several classes attending and participating in many programs on subjects pertaining to conservation and nature. Each presenter would have five classes for 20 minutes each to teach about their diversified subjects. In the last two years, I have included five minutes telling the students about the litter problem and passing out litter bags, stickers and flyers, which developed into the Green Team.

The Green Team is a group of volunteers working to educate citizens and reduce litter in our beautiful county. In creating the team and finding direction, I had the opportunity of talking to the Superintendent of Fulton Schools, Bill Lynch. One Sunday morning at a Rotary fundraising breakfast, I asked him what the possibilities were of talking to school children about the litter problem. Bill was very agreeable and told me to let Carrie Spawn, a school nurse, who I worked out with at the YMCA. In addition,

Bill would set up a meeting with his staff and Dan Mainville, an Environmental Science teacher, and Jerry Siegal, Head of Grounds to discuss the program.

Bill proceeded to have me attend school assemblies to talk to the children and pass out the litter bags for their parents that we had purchased through Oswego County Tourism. Dan joined the Green Team and took on the responsibility of presentations to school children. His Environmental Team actually donated $40 to our Green Team that they'd earned through their recycling program. Through their program, Dan pointed out how they earn money and had purchased water fountains with double spigots, one for drinking and the other for refilling plastic bottles for their use.

After a time, Dan became more involved with his own curriculum and required duties and our team has since taken over calling on school children. Thanks to our team member, Steve Osborne, who took the bull by the horn and revised our PowerPoint for this program, making it more practical for any of us to use with the program. At our last meeting of the year, I invited Deputy Sherriff Cristy Crast to become a team member and she accepted. I had met her at Patty Ritchie's Senior Health Fair recently in Oswego, which I attended to receive my award as "Senior Citizen of the Year" from the Senator. I had time on my hands that day while waiting for the Senator, so I spent that time going to all the booths telling everyone about our Green Team, its purpose and handing out bags and flyers. That's where I met Deputy Crast and she became very interested in our cause. Our team is looking forward to working with her.

The current Green Team membership is myself, Sandy, Betty Mauté, Steve Osborne, Dick Drosse, Paula Rohn, Deputy Craft and Jim Farfaglia. Steve Chirello, of Chirello Advertising, is not on the team, but contributed a large supply of printed barrel and waste can labels, saving us a lot of money.

Early in May 2017, I was invited to Albany by the Office For The Aging (OFA) to receive recognition for all my past volunteerism including starting the Green Team Anti-Litter group. I chose not to go to Albany, but was recognized for this later at a County Legislative meeting. The gentleman in charge of the OFA presented me with a certificate of recognition for all of this.

In the early part of August, I was visiting Terry Wilbur, assistant to Assemblyman Barclay, at their office and was informed by Jennifer Cook, Chief of Staff, that I was to receive recognition as a follow-up on August 18, 2017 at 3:00pm in Barclay's chambers. They told me I could invite anyone I wanted, up to 20 in number. They took care of inviting Green Team members and Oswego County Tourism members. I ended up inviting family and friends that were able to attend. We all gathered in the room and introductions were made.

Before everything got started, Assemblyman Barclay asked Father Fuchs to offer the blessing. Father Fuchs later came up to tell his experience as a friend over the years and how we used to do weightlifting in our high school years and how he was sweet on my sister Edith at the time. Father Fuchs was in the Army during World War II and was assigned as a bodyguard to the judge at the Nuremburg Nazi trials after the war. Just this year, he was invited back to Nuremburg to celebrate the anniversary of the trials as a city guest along with one other survivor. He still celebrates mass here in Fulton every day at 94 years of age.

Assemblyman Barclay started out by telling the purpose of honoring me for all I had contributed to the community as a senior citizen. He pulled up a two-page wide plaque and proceeded to read it to the audience. I accepted it proudly, but humbly. There were several pictures taken with Assemblyman Barclay and then with family. After that, he invited anyone to come up and add their input. First was Janet Clerkin, Tourism and Public Information Coordinator, who explained how the Green Team got started, which pleased me.

Fran Verdoliva, Salmon Fish Hatchery, got up and told them how for seven years in the fall on National Fishing Day, I participated with my display of my canoes and how they were built. I participated by setting up my boats and boat building display outside a lean-to, near the back exit. One of the days while we had the boats on display, I noticed a lady, Loretta Lipkowski, who told me she was a local artist and was painting my boat scene. This was to be auctioned off that evening and the proceeds given to the

Art Association. I attended the auction and bid on it, but backed out at the high price. After I got home, Sandy gave me the dickens for letting it slip by. Later, I contacted the artist to see if she could do another scene from her memory. She said yes, so I contracted her to do it. I was pleasantly surprised that she was able to do this.

After the program was all over I had an opportunity to explain to Barclay the need to create public awareness by getting the message on public TV on a routine basis, the same as with the Recycling Program that is already being shown. Barclay suggested I come to Albany to do a 15-minute anti-litter program on his TV station. I am hoping this will happen as it would be a tremendous opportunity for our cause. Since then, we recently met with Fran Verdoliva at the Hatchery, where he made a video with my two neighbor girls and myself showing aspects of his anti-litter program there. He has since been editing it and when satisfied he will burn it in to his video program at the Hatchery for the public to view for awareness.

Last year, Patty Ritchie had a Senior Health Fair in Oswego and invited me to be there at a certain time. Sandy and I went there at that time, Patty started the program addressing the crowd and then called me up, presenting me with an award for Senior Citizen of the Year for all that I had done. We had our picture taken, I thanked her for it and for all she does for the county and Veterans.

At this point of my life, I plan to continue efforts of the Green

Team to stop litter in Oswego County. It has been over two and a half years since we started this program. I have a second guide boat partially finished that I hope to get at. I plan to plank the second one using a wide board, screws and tacks, which is the traditional method old time boat builders use. I laminated the ribs instead of using ribs made from cured spruce stumps, where the old timers took advantage of the natural curve to form them. The problem is the cost of buying the stumps called flitches which selects stumps with a natural curve.

As time goes by, I plan to continue on with my daily activities which include YMCA Board Member, TAC Board Member and Chairman of the Oswego County Anti-Litter Campaign. I also plan to continue YMCA daily workout and Granby pool swim program three times a week. Sandy and I plan to continue living in our two-story executive colonial and eventually scale down to a one-story ranch or renting a one-story condominium.

I hope you've enjoyed the story of my life up to this point.

Acknowledgements

I wish to acknowledge that certain people gave me help in writing this story:

Jim Farfaglia. Jim encouraged me to write this book, and he edited it.

Betty Mauté. Betty did all the tireless hours of typing and gathering my photos. On a humorous note during our typing session, I said to her you must be getting bored and she said, "Oh no, I can't wait to get to the end of the sentences."

Janet Clerkin. Janet listened to ideas of forming an anti-litter team for Oswego County. We started out as a subcommittee of Tourism Advisory Council (TAC), but later became independent. She has stayed on our team as a very valuable member particularly as an advisor. She also did an article, "Bob Builds Boats," in which she told all about my boat building and showing them. She included Jim Farfaglia's story about my working with young folks at Camp Hollis.

Fran Verdoliva of the Salmon River Hatchery. At our November 2014 TAC meeting in Richland, Fran covered the litter problem and how public interest had dropped off with littering signs gone. It was then that I came up with the anti-littering problem. I was frustrated almost every day picking up litter on my lawn. I realized that someone had to do something about it so I did! He has also invited me every year on National Fishing Day to set up my boats at the lean to as a public service on boat building.

My wife Sandy. Sandy is a tireless help manning the Green Team Committee, sending and receiving communications. She now runs the meetings. She also provides her special touch to all our holiday gatherings, making each event special for all attendees.

Erica Schreiner. After we started the Green Team, Erica, who is the Senior District Technician for the Oswego County Soil & Water Conservation District, arranged for me to talk with several Oswego County Environmental Club schoolteachers who have an interest in controlling litter. Erica was also instrumental in opening an account for our finances. Also helping with this is her office's Treasurer, Cindy Williams.

Morris Sorbello. Morris has been a great supporter of my efforts since I started the anti-litter campaign. He has taken opportunities to speak of my efforts and point out that I should have more recognition. He pointed this out when I received my award from Will Barclay.

Father Moritz Fuchs. Father Fuchs paid tribute to me, telling about how we were in school together.

During my life, I've had the privilege to meet many people and have had the opportunity to learn from them and share my life experiences. I apologize if I've left anyone out of this book.

Made in the USA
Columbia, SC
11 March 2018